ON THE SHOULDERS OF GIANTS

THE HISTORY OF SCIENCE FROM THE ANCIENT GREEKS TO THE SCIENTIFIC REVOLUTION

Ray Spangenburg and Diane K. Moser

Facts On File

The History of Science from the Ancient Greeks to the Scientific Revolution

Facts On File, Inc.
460 Park Avenue South
New York NY 10016
USA

Library of Congress Cataloging-in-Publication Data

Spangenburg, Ray, 1939–
    The history of science from the ancient Greeks to the scientific revolution / Ray Spangenburg and Diane K. Moser.
        p.   cm.—(On the shoulders of giants)
    Includes bibliographical references and index.
    Summary: Surveys the early history of science, discussing the philosophical underpinnings developed by Greek thinkers, continuing through the developments of the Middle Ages and the Renaissance, and concluding with the discoveries of the seventeenth century.
    ISBN 0-8160-2739-0
    1. Science—History—Juvenile literature.   [1. Science—History.]
I. Moser, Diane, 1944– . II. Title. III. Series: Spangenburg, Ray, 1939–   On the shoulders of giants.
Q126.4.H57   1993   92-33180
509—dc20

A British CIP catalogue record for this book is available from the British Library.

Facts On File books are available at special discounts when purchased in bulk quantities for businesses, associations, institutions or sales promotions. Please call our Special Sales Department in New York at 212/683-2244 (dial 800/322-8755 except in NY).

Text design by Ron Monteleone
Cover design by Semadar Megged
Composition by Facts On File, Inc.
Manufactured by the Maple-Vail Book Manufacturing Group
Printed in the United States of America

10 9 8 7 6 5 4 3 2 1

This book is printed on acid-free paper.

C O N T E N T S

A C K N O W L E D G M E N T S

So many people have been generous with their time, talents and expertise in helping us with this book, both as we wrote it and in the past when it was only a dream. We would like to thank them all—and especially: For their help with illustrations, Dr. Owen Gingerich of Harvard University, Andrew Fraknoi of the Astronomical Society of the Pacific, Leslie Overstreet of the Smithsonian Institution Libraries, Diane Vogt-O'Connor of the Smithsonian Archives, Jan Lazarus of the National Library of Medicine, Clark Evans of the Library of Congress, R. W. Errickson of Parke-Davis, Cynthia M. Serve of Bausch & Lomb, and R. M. Edmund of Edmund Scientific; for kindly reading the manuscript and making many insightful suggestions, Beth Etgen, educational director at the Sacramento Science Center, and her staff, as well as science historian Karl Kall; and for meticulous attention to detail, copy editor Janet S. McDonald. Thanks also to our excellent editors at Facts On File, Nicole Bowen and James Warren, for their many helpful suggestions. And to many others, including Jeanne Sheldon-Parsons, Laurie Wise, Chris McKay of NASA Ames, Robert Sheaffer and Bob Steiner, for many long conversations about science, its history and its purpose.

To Pat and John Nappi, whose friendship, support and patience listening to the enthusiasms and frustrations of the writing life often verge on the heroic

P R E F A C E   T O
T H E   S E R I E S

. . . our eyes once opened, . . . we can never go back to the old outlook. . . .
But in each revolution of scientific thought new words are set to the old
music, and that which has gone before is not destroyed but refocused.
—A. S. Eddington

What is science? How is it different from other ways of thinking? And what are scientists like? How do they think and what do they mean when they talk about "doing science"?

Science isn't just test tubes or strange apparatus. And it's not just frog dissections or names of plant species. Science is a way of thinking, a vital, ever-growing way of looking at the world. It is a way of discovering how the

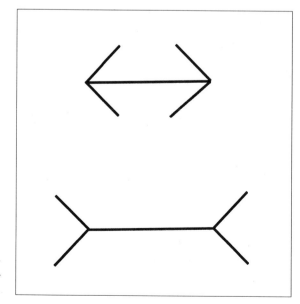

Looks can be deceiving:
These two lines are the
same length.

world works—a very particular way that uses a set of rules devised by scientists to help them also discover their own mistakes.

Everyone knows how easy it is to make a mistake about what one sees or hears or perceives in any way. If you don't believe it, look at the two horizontal lines on page vi. One looks like a two-way arrow; the other has the arrow heads inverted. Which one do you think is longer (not including the "arrow heads")? Now measure them both. Right, they are exactly the same length. Because it's so easy to go wrong in making observations and drawing conclusions, people developed a system, a "scientific method," for asking "How can I be sure?" If you actually took the time to measure the two lines in our example, instead of just taking our word that both lines are the same length, then you were thinking like a scientist. You were testing your own observation. You were testing the information that we had given you that both lines "are exactly the same length." And, you were employing one of the strongest tools of science to do your test: you were quantifying, or measuring, the lines.

More than 2,000 years ago Aristotle, a Greek philosopher, told the world that when two objects of different weights were dropped from a height the heaviest would hit the ground first. It was a common-sense argument. After all, anyone who wanted to try a test could make an "observation" and see that if you dropped a leaf and a stone together the stone would land first. Try it yourself with a sheet of notebook paper and a paperweight in your living room. Not many Greeks tried such a test though. Why bother when the answer was already known? And, being philosophers who believed in the power of the human mind to simply "reason" such things out without having to resort to "tests," they considered such an activity to be intellectually and socially unacceptable.

Centuries later, Galileo Galilei, a brilliant Italian who liked to figure things out for himself, did run some tests. Galileo, though, like today's scientists, wasn't content merely to observe the objects fall. Using two balls of different weights, a time-keeping device, and an inclined plane, or ramp, he allowed the balls to roll down the ramp and carefully *measured* their movement. And, he did this not once, but many times, inclining planes at many different angles. His results, which still offend the common sense of many people today, demonstrated that, if you discount air resistance, all objects released at the same time from the same height would hit the ground at the same time. In a perfect vacuum (which couldn't be created in Galileo's time), all objects would fall at the same rate! You can run a rough test of this yourself (although it is by no means a really accurate experiment), by crumpling the notebook paper into a ball and then dropping it at the same time as the paperweight.

Galileo's experiments (which he carefully recorded step by step) and his conclusions based on these experiments demonstrate another important attribute of science. Anyone who wanted to could duplicate the experiments, and either verify his results or, by looking for flaws or errors in the experiments, prove him partially or wholly incorrect. No one ever proved Galileo wrong. And years later when it was possible to create a vacuum (even though his experiments had been accurate enough to win everybody over long before that), his conclusions passed the test.

Galileo had not only shown that Aristotle had been wrong. He demonstrated how, by observation, experiment and quantification, Aristotle, if he had so wished, might have proven himself wrong—and thus changed his own opinion! Above all else the scientific way of thinking is a way to keep yourself from fooling yourself—or from letting nature (or others) fool you.

Of course, science is more than observation, experimentation and presentation of results. No one today can read a newspaper or a magazine without becoming quickly aware of the fact that science is always bubbling with "theories." "Astronomer at X Observatory Has Found Startling New Evidence that Throws into Question Einstein's Theory of Relativity," says a magazine. "School System in the State of Y Condemns Books that Unquestioningly Accept Darwin's Theory of Evolution," says a newspaper. "Bizarre New Results in Quantum Theory Say that You May Not Exist!" shouts another paper. What is this thing called "theory"?

Few scientists pretend anymore that they have the completely "detached" and objective "scientific method" proposed by the philosopher Francis Bacon and others at the dawn of the scientific revolution in the 17th century. This "method," in its simplest form, proposed that in attempting to answer the questions put forward by nature, the investigator into nature's secrets must objectively and without preformed opinions observe, experiment and gather data about the phenomena. "I make no hypotheses," Isaac Newton announced after demonstrating the universal law of gravity when it was suggested that he might have an idea *what gravity was.* Historians have noted that Newton apparently did have a couple of ideas, or "hypotheses," as to the possible nature of gravity, but for the most part he kept these private. As far as Newton was concerned there had already been enough hypothesizing and too little attention paid to the careful gathering of testable facts and figures.

Today, though, we know that scientists don't always follow along the simple and neat pathways laid out by the trail guide called the "scientific method." Sometimes, either before or after experiments, a scientist will get an idea or a hunch (that is, a somewhat less than well thought out hypothesis) that suggests a new approach or a different way of looking at a problem. Then he or she will run experiments and gather data to attempt to prove or disprove this hypothesis. Sometimes the word *hypothesis* is used more loosely in everyday conversation, but for a hypothesis to be valid scientifically it must have built within it some way that it can be proven wrong if, in fact, it is wrong. That is, it must be falsifiable.

Not all scientists actually run experiments themselves. Most theoreticians, for instance, map out their arguments mathematically. But hypotheses, to be taken seriously by the scientific community, must always carry with them the seeds of falsifiability by experiment and observation.

To become a theory a hypothesis has to pass several tests. It has to hold up under experiments, not just by one scientist conducting the experiments or making the observations, but to others performing other experiments and observations as well. Then when thoroughly reinforced by continual testing and appraising, the hypothesis may become known to the scientific or popular world as a "theory."

It is important to remember that even a theory is also subject to falsification or correction. A good theory, for instance, will make "predictions"—events that its testers can look for as a further test of its validity. By the time most well-known theories such as Einstein's theory of relativity or Darwin's theory of evolution reach the textbook stage, they have survived the gamut of verification to the extent that they have become productive working tools for other scientists. But in science, no theory can be accepted as completely "proven"; it must remain always open to further tests and scrutiny as new facts or observations emerge. It is this insistently self-correcting nature of science that makes it both the most demanding and the most productive of humankind's attempts to understand the workings of nature. This kind of critical thinking is the key element of doing science.

The cartoon-version scientist portrayed as a bespectacled, rigid man in a white coat, certain of his own infallibility, couldn't be farther from reality. Scientists, both men and women, are as human as the rest of us—and they come in all races, sizes and appearances, with and without eyeglasses. As a group, because their methodology focuses so specifically on fallibility and critical thinking, they are probably even more aware than the rest of us of how easy it is to be wrong. But they like being right whenever possible, and they like working toward finding the right answers to questions. That's usually why they became scientists.

This book and the four others in this series, On the Shoulders of Giants, look at how people have developed this system for finding out how the world works, making use of both success and failure. We will look at the theories scientists put forth, sometimes right and sometimes wrong. And we will look at how we have learned to test, accept and build upon those theories—or to correct, expand or simplify them.

We'll also see how scientists have learned from others' mistakes, sometimes having to discard theories that once seemed logical but later proved to be incorrect, misleading, too limited or unfruitful. In all these ways they have built upon the shoulders of the men and women of science, the giants, who went before them.

PRECURSORS OF SCIENCE: FROM ANCIENT TIMES TO THE MIDDLE AGES

CHAPTER 1

LEGACIES FROM ANCIENT PEOPLES

*I*t was as if someone suddenly opened a window and let the fresh air pour into a long-closed and musty room. Nearly 2,500 years ago, as the fresh Mediterranean air breezed along the sun-drenched buildings of the seaports of ancient Greece, people began to look at the world differently than they ever had before. What was this new outlook of the ancient Greeks—this remarkable break from the views of the past?

Today when we refer to the most famous of the early Greek thinkers we call them *philosophers*, based on the original meaning of the word, those who love and search for knowledge or wisdom. The tremendous contribution made by these thinkers was the belief that ordinary human beings could hope to understand the workings of nature. As basic as this belief seems to us today, it was a momentous and heroic act of self-confidence on the part of the early Greeks. It was the first glimmer of science—not as we know it today, but its precursor. Those preceding them had never even dreamed that the human mind could venture into this territory, once believed to be governed by the capricious whims of spirits and gods.

What emboldened the Greek philosophers to take such an audacious step? Why, at that particular point in human history, did they make this tremendous shift in perspective that opened up the doors of knowledge? Who were their precursors, how did they set the stage and how were the Greeks different?

BEFORE THE GREEKS: MEASUREMENT AND MYTHOLOGY

Far back in time, long before any civilization for which we have records, the first humans began asking basic questions about the world around them.

3

Questions such as: What are those points of light in the night sky? What is night and why is it different from day? Why does a tree fall? What is fire and why does it burn? Why does smoke rise and wood become ash? What is a human and what is an animal and how are they different? How do some plants sustain life when eaten, while others are poisonous? What is life? What is death? Is a stone alive?

And they began to devise answers based on what they thought they saw. The earliest, most primitive answers explained most natural events—the seasons, the wind, the growing of plants, the flooding of rivers—in terms of spirits. Spirits, though not seen, were thought to dwell everywhere in nature—in rocks, in the wind, in the clouds, in the river. Like people, they could be happy, angry, sad or jealous. A river flooded because the river spirit or god was angry and wanted to punish. Spirits also could be flattered or persuaded or cajoled: Rain came to water the fields because the rain gods were pleased or had been appeased.

Throughout the long dawn of humankind's history most views of the world were of this spiritual or mythological kind. People developed systems for trying to influence the world around them—to cure illness, end droughts, win wars or prevent floods—by using magic to call on the spirits or gods. They used incantations and potions. They tried to read signs by examining dead animals' livers. They made sacrifices. And sometimes, due to coincidences, these methods seemed to work. Whenever they worked, the spiritual view of the world was reinforced. When they didn't work, people tended to think they'd done the potion or incantation wrong rather than disbelieve that spirits were at work.

But, at the same time, ancient peoples began developing other tools to control the world around them—tools that worked more reliably. During the Old Stone Age (possibly as long ago as 2.4 million years), they began to fashion materials and make weapons for hunting. By Neolithic times, or the New Stone Age (about 6,000 to 10,000 years ago), they understood enough about how plants grew to be able to plant and grow their own food, and agriculture was born. These advances were purely practical—technological, not scientific—but they were some of the earliest examples of people using logic and putting ideas together to understand some small part of the world.

Large-scale agriculture began when, about the fourth millennium B.C., the Sumerians in the Tigris-Euphrates River valley first hooked animals up to a plow and to wheeled carts. These people also built ships, which meant they soon needed to devise methods of navigation across the seas. By 5,000 years ago the Sumerians were combining copper and tin to make bronze, and metallurgy was born. The Egyptians on the Nile, meanwhile, were making many of the same advancements.

By this time urban civilizations existed in the areas around the perimeter of the Mediterranean, and trade and agriculture had become complex enough that records had to be kept. Both the Sumerians and the Egyptians developed numeric systems and methods of keeping accounts, a job that was entrusted to priest-administrators. The Sumerians developed a cuneiform method of writing on clay tablets, and the Egyptians used hieroglyphs on papyrus. They developed mathematical tables: multiplication, division, squared numbers and square roots.

By about 4,000 years ago another tribe, the Babylonians, ascended to power in Mesopotamia. Much of the calendar system we use today was conceived by the Babylonians, based on their close observations of the Sun, Moon and planets. Their motivations were both practical and spiritual. On the practical side, they needed a way to keep track of time—to anticipate the changes in seasons and the flooding of rivers. Their spiritual interest came from their belief in a system known as astrology that supposed that the positions of the planets controlled people's lives. The Babylonians' observations of the night sky, given the tools they had to use, were amazingly accurate and served as stepping stones for astronomers to come.

All of this, too, strictly speaking, was technology, not science—the development of tools and methods for bettering human life, not knowledge for the sake of knowledge. But, in developing these technologies, people were developing the tools that later generations, even thousands of years later, would use to search for answers about how the world worked.

Today we take so many of these tools completely for granted that it's easy to overlook the extraordinary progress these early peoples made. Any 10-year-old can recite a multiplication table. But how many of us could come up with a numerical system that worked? (One proof of the difficulty is the fact that both the Romans and the Egyptians came up with systems that made multiplying and dividing very awkward. Try multiplying VII by XXXII.) The first person to create bronze or smelt iron had to have come upon the process as the result of experimentation, observation and thinking. In Central America, early peoples discovered that they could remove the poison from the cassava plant and use its tuberous roots, once freed of the poison, for food. To make this discovery, these people, too, must have gone through a process of investigation and use of logic—some of the same processes that science would come to rely on.

But the birth of science was still a long way off. Up to the end of the Bronze Age (about 5,500 to 3,000 years ago) no people had gone beyond developing practical intellectual tools, systems and technologies for managing the civilizations they had built. Some, like the Babylonians, had made excellent observations and calculations in the service of astrology. But all of them still made magic an important part of their world view and none of them asked why or looked for natural causes.

Then a combination of circumstances and events made it possible for an entirely different point of view to develop. By about 3,300 years ago

Replica of a Babylonian tablet (Smithsonian Institution, photo #64196)

alphabets were born in Phoenicia (one based on the Babylonian cuneiform system, the other on Egyptian hieroglyphics) and writing as well as reading were simplified, enabling people other than trained priests to communicate by the written word. Also, sometime after about 4,000 years ago, in the Armenian mountains, a group of people developed an efficient method to smelt iron out of iron ore. As the method of smelting iron became more prevalent, by about 1,000 years later, some of these tribes to the north gained military strength (among them a group known as the Dorian Greeks) and began conquering the civilizations of the high Bronze Age.

THE ANCIENT GREEKS: NEW WAYS OF LOOKING AT THINGS

The collection of tribes known as the Dorian Greeks flowed down in waves from the northwest and north central mainland into the Macedonian peninsula (the area now known as Greece) and the eastern Mediterranean.

Because of the isolation of the communities they formed, hundreds of independent city-states came into existence over the following centuries. These city-states were loosely associated but were left free to form their own governments and subcultures. No central authority dictated philosophy, and, while priests and priestesses were consulted for predictions and wisdom, they did not have the far-reaching economic and political power that their counterparts held elsewhere.

The Macedonian peninsula, with its many inlets and nearby islands, lent itself readily to the development of a seafaring economy, and the Greeks traveled, traded and colonized widely. They developed a keen spatial sense of the world around them—the kind of geometric mind-set that comes with navigation and travel. And they soon discovered that world views differed vastly from one corner of the Mediterranean to another. Some of what they saw seemed useful to them, and some didn't—but uncommitted as they were, they were free to choose the ideas and systems that seemed to work best and discard what did not.

Like other ancient civilizations, the Greeks had developed an elaborate mythology, peopled with gods, goddesses, nymphs, fates, muses and other inhabitants of a spirit world. But, unlike some other cultures, they saw their gods as fallible (though larger than life) and neither all-powerful nor all-knowing. As a result, Greek thinkers were perhaps less inclined to use supernatural explanations and more apt, because of their experience with the seas and other civilizations, to look for natural causes.

So, given the Greeks' lack of a central authority governing the city-states, their exposure to other cultures, and the relative openness of their own mythological system, they were ripe for a new way of looking at the world. But it was also curiosity that led the Greeks to make the transition from reliance on myth to a search for knowledge. They sought to find general patterns in nature, to find order. "Why" seemed like a good question to the Greeks because it helped to open their eyes, to look for these patterns and generalizations that would help them see order behind all the apparent variations.

Not everything about the way the Greeks looked at the world was productive. As we'll see, thinkers for many generations after the Greeks often followed too closely in their footsteps. Most of the Greek philosophers relied too heavily on subjective thought and intellectual exercises and too little on observation or experiment. Their concepts originated primarily within their minds: They developed ideas about how nature should work and then they tried to fit nature to their ideas.

But they gave us the first gateway into a world of natural causes, a world that could be explored and explained, that people could understand—a world revealed through simple analogies, not religious dogma or superstition. The Egyptians, Babylonians and others who had gone before had developed mathematical tools, observed and tabulated events and kept records. But their approach was more like accounting and they directed most of their efforts toward keeping records. The Greeks were different. They wanted to look behind the facts for the causes—and they were the first to look consistently for natural, not supernatural, causes and to build a cosmology on that premise. This single shift would completely transform the way people looked at the world.

Thales

We don't know much about the earliest Greek philosophers. The best known, Thales of Miletus, is thought to have been born sometime around 624 B.C. and to have lived in the Ionian city of Miletus on the coast of Anatolia, today the west coast of Turkey. Most of what we know about Thales [THAY-leez] comes from the writing of Aristotle and other Greek philosophers who lived a couple of hundred years later. It's believed that Thales was a merchant and businessman who traveled widely and probably spent some time in Egypt. Thales is particularly important because he is thought to be the first of the Greek philosophers to move away from supernatural explanations in trying to understand the nature of the world. Thales's thinking about the *nature* of nature led him to speculate on one of the oldest of all scientific questions: What is the world made of? His conclusion, although it may seem somewhat naive to us today, is important, not only because it represents an attempt to see the physical makeup of the world as something that could be understood, but also because Thales attempted to see each part of the world as systematically integrated with the rest of it. The Earth, Thales said, floats on water, and all the parts of it, everything that makes it up, from its mountains and plains to its air and sky, its trees and creatures, were also composed of different states or forms of water. Thales's idea turned out to be incorrect. But by asking the question and then trying to answer it, he leaped the chasm separating the old mythological ways of seeing the world and arrived, the first known traveler, in today's world of science and knowledge.

The Milesian School

Like most of the great Greek philosophers, Thales had an influence on others around him. His two best-known followers, although there were undoubtedly others who attained less renown, were Anaximander and Anaximenes. Both were also from Miletus and so, like Thales, are known as members of the Milesian School. Much more is known about Anaximander than about Anaximenes, probably because Anaximander [a-NAK-si-man-der], who was born sometime around 610 B.C., ambitiously attempted to write a comprehensive history of the universe. As would later happen between another teacher-student pair, Plato and Aristotle, Anaximander disagreed with his teacher despite his respect for him. He doubted that the world and all its contents could be made of water and proposed instead a formless and unobservable substance he called apeiron that was the source of all matter. Anaximander's most important contributions, though, were in other areas. Although he did not accept that water was the prime element, he did believe that all life originated in the sea, and he was thus one of the first to conceive of this important idea. Anaximander is credited with drawing up the first world map of the Greeks and also with recognizing that the Earth's surface was curved. He believed, though, that the shape of the Earth was that of a cylinder, rather than the sphere that later Greek philosophers would conjecture. Anaximander, observing the motions of the heavens around the pole star, was probably the first of the Greek philosophers to picture the sky as a sphere completely surrounding the Earth—an idea that, elaborated upon later, would cause enormous complications in astronomy until the advent of the scientific revolution in the 17th century.

Unfortunately most of Anaximander's written history of the universe was lost, and only a few fragments survive today. Little is known about his other ideas. Unfortunately, too, most of the written work of Anaximenes, who may have been Anaximander's pupil, has also been lost. All that we can say for certain about Anaximenes [AN-ak-SIM-ih-neez], who was probably born around 570 B.C., is that following in the tradition of Anaximander, he also disagreed with his mentor. The world, according to Anaximenes, was not composed of either water or apeiron, but air itself was the fundamental element of the universe. Compressed, it became water and earth, and when rarefied or thinned out it heated up to become fire. Not much else is known about Anaximenes, but he may have also been the first to study rainbows and speculate upon their natural rather than supernatural cause. He is thought to have been the first Greek to distinguish the differences between the planets, identifying, for instance, the separate identities of Mars and Venus.

With the door opened by Thales and the other early philosophers of Miletus, Greek thinkers began to speculate about the nature of the universe. It's important to remember, though, that this exciting burst of intellectual activity was for the most part purely creative. The Greeks, from Thales to Plato and Aristotle, were philosophers and not scientists. It is possible for anyone to create "ideas" about the nature and structure of the universe for instance, and many times these ideas can be so consistent and elaborately structured, or just so apparently "obvious," that they can be persuasive to many people. A "scientific" theory about the universe, however, demands much more than the various observations and analogies that were woven together to form systems of reasoning, carefully constructed as they were, that would eventually culminate in Aristotle's model of the world. The bottom line was that without experimentation and objective and critical testing of their theories—concepts unknown to the Greeks—the best that they could hope to achieve was some internally consistent speculation that covered all the bases and satisfied the demands of reason.

Pythagoras

"All things are numbers," Pythagoras once said. And despite some mystical and bizarre beliefs he held about numbers, we owe him a major debt for his insistence that through mathematics we could get a grip on understanding the world.

Born in Samos sometime around 560 B.C., Pythagoras [pih-THAG-oh-rus] was a brilliant and eccentric mathematician, philosopher and religious leader who had migrated to Croton in what is now southern Italy and founded a cult devoted to mathematics and mysticism. It's difficult today to disentangle what was actually said and believed by Pythagoras and what was invented by his followers. The famous Pythagorean Theorem, so familiar in geometry classes—that the square of the hypotenuse of a right triangle is equal to the sum of the squares of the other two sides—may have been proved by him or by one of his followers. But such was the secret nature of the cult that the origin of even this major achievement is difficult to trace. Pythagoras, however, is generally credited with establishing the idea of geometry as a logically connected sequence of propositions.

Speculating about the nature of the universe, Pythagoras taught that the center of the world was not the Earth but a central fire around which the Earth moved. We couldn't see this central fire, said Pythagoras, because our side of the Earth always points away from it. The light from the Sun, however, was a reflection of that fire. The Earth itself, said the Pythagoreans, was a sphere and it was surrounded by a spherical universe. The Pythagoreans also pointed out that the Sun, Moon and planets moved separately and differently than the stars and were obviously at different distances from the Earth. The movements of the planets as well as the stars, the Pythagoreans believed, formed perfect uniform circles, following the most beautiful and perfect geometric form. Ironically, although they had correctly discerned the separate nature of the stars and planets, it was their belief in the circular motion of the heavenly bodies and the spherical shape of the universe surrounding the Earth that would help lead astronomy into many confusions that would remain until the 17th century.

Not all the thoughts of the intellectually questing Greeks were turned toward the nature of matter and the form of the heavens. Alcmaeon [alk-MEE-on], born in Croton sometime around 530 B.C., was a follower of

Pythagoras whose interest had turned to medicine. Since the Greeks had a healthy interest in medicine as well as a tendency toward hypochondria, there was a great deal of work for a good physician, and policies about how one could go about practicing the craft of medicine were fairly liberal. Although superstition still played a major role in the practice of those physicians who treated the poor and less privileged classes, many Greek physicians had turned toward a more realistic and practical study and treatment.

While he shared some of the mystical notions of the Pythagoreans, Alcmaeon is reported to have been among the first to perform dissections of human and animal bodies for the sole purpose of anatomical research. He reported the existence of the optic nerve within the eye and the tube (now called the Eustachian tube) connecting the ear and mouth. He may have recognized the differences between veins and arteries, and his medical studies convinced him that the brain was probably the center of the intellect, an idea that would not be accepted until much later.

Heraclitus

It was inevitable that all this study into "natural philosophy," or the study of nature, should set some Greeks pondering about what all of this meant to the average human being. Heraclitus [her-uh-KLY-tus], born about 540 B.C. near Miletus, earned himself the nickname "the weeping philosopher" because of his pessimistic view that nothing in life was permanent and that everything was always in a state of change, leaving nothing that anyone could count on. The primary element, said Heraclitus, was fire, itself ever changing and enforcing change on all other things. Even the Sun, according to Heraclitus, was not the Sun seen yesterday, but a new and different one that would itself be gone tomorrow to be replaced by yet another.

Anaxagoras

Anaxagoras, born also near Miletus sometime around 500 B.C., had a much less dispirited view of the cosmos. The last of the great philosophers to come from the Ionian tradition of Thales, Anaxagoras [an-ak-ZAG-oh-rus] took his teachings to Athens sometime around 460 B.C. A dedicated rationalist who opposed mysticism in any form, be it the old mysticism of the gods or the newer mysticism of the Pythagoreans, Anaxagoras would also become the first major philosopher to suffer persecution for his views.

The Sun, he believed, was a gigantic red-hot stone and the Moon was illuminated by the reflected light of the hot Sun. In a view that shocked many of his contemporaries who praised the perfection and purity of the heavens, he also suggested that the Moon itself was much like the Earth, complete with mountains and valleys, and might even be inhabited. He also

11

explained, quite accurately, the phases of the Moon as well as the eclipses of both the Sun and the Moon in terms of the movements of those bodies. The stars and planets, he said, were flaming rocks much like the Sun.

This was heady stuff in Athens, which was religiously conservative, and to top it all off, Anaxagoras also taught that the universe had not been created by deities but had been born out of a chaos of "seeds" brought into order by some kind of rotation by an abstract "mind." Thus, he explained, all the heavenly bodies were brought into being at the same time as the Earth, and therefore the Earth and heavens were composed of the same materials.

This was too much, even though the Greeks had grown accustomed to such intellectual speculation from their philosophers. Perhaps much could be explained by the philosophers, but the Greeks still believed in their gods and perfect heavens. After 30 years of teaching and helping to earn Athens its reputation as the intellectual center of Greece, Anaxagoras was brought to trial for impiety.

The trial didn't last long. With the help of some influential friends speaking up for him, he was acquitted. It was the end of an era, however. Fearing that he might be prosecuted again, Anaxagoras fled Athens to the countryside, where he died six years later. Although a few of his students remained to pursue the problems of natural philosophy, the philosophical tone of Athens shifted away from the mysteries of nature. Under the guidance of Socrates (born approximately 470 B.C.), thinkers began to probe instead the problems of human conduct and moral philosophy.

Rationalists and Atomists

Outside Athens natural philosophy continued to flourish. One of the more intriguing schools to emerge from the great burst of intellectual activity that characterized ancient Greece was the one begun by Democritus, born about 470 B.C. Democritus [de-MOK-rih-tus], who had picked up the seeds of his ideas from his teacher, Leucippus (c. 490 B.C.–?), about whom little is known, put forth a view of the universe that, although based on pure imagination and speculation, was strikingly modern in many aspects.

Democritus agreed with some of the other rationalists that the Moon was probably a body with mountains and valleys much like Earth. And he speculated that the Milky Way was very likely an immense collection of stars. More important though was his speculation that the world and everything in it, including human beings, was composed of collections of infinitesimal and invisible particles that were hard and unbreakable. These atoms, as he called them (from the Greek *atomos*, meaning "indivisible") had shape, mass and motion as they moved through empty space. Other qualities such as smell, color or flavor were imposed on them by observers. He also argued that the universe itself had come into being out of a vast, spinning vortex of such atoms, and that an infinite number of worlds had been created in the same manner.

The atoms, according to Democritus's theory, were indestructible, eternal and unchanging. All change in matter was simply the coming apart or the coming together of masses of joined atoms. Furthermore, said Democritus, even the human mind and, more shockingly, the gods, if they existed, were composed of such atoms.

It was a good theory, as we know now, but the problem was that, like all the other Greek theories, it was pure speculation. And, with no way to prove or disprove it, atomism carried no heavier weight than any of the dozens of other theories that were floating around Greece at the time. In addition, one major strike against it in public opinion was that such a purely mechanistic view of the universe left absolutely no room or reason for the existence of gods. This aspect of atomism became even clearer during the following century in the writings of the philosopher Epicurus (born in 341 B.C.). In his own time Democritus, who had little patience for superstition, had also argued against an afterlife and believed that the human conscience should be the sole arbitrator of right or wrong in human actions. It was a point that Epicurus [ep-ih-KYOO-rus] would pound home in the fourth century B.C., and which failed to endear either Democritus in his time or Epicurus in his to their religious or conservative contemporaries. Atomism had few fans either before or after Epicurus other than the Roman philosopher and poet Lucretius (born in Rome about 95 B.C.), and Democritus's atomic theory was destined to lie dormant until its revival by John Dalton in the 19th century.

Aristotle—And "Why Things Happen"

For science, by far the most significant of all Greek philosophers was Aristotle. A man of vast curiosity and wide-ranging intellect, he developed concepts on a grander scale than anyone before him. He was the first thinker on record anywhere to conceive of an integrated system to explain how all aspects of the universe worked. He got a lot of things wrong—and his theories had many holes that later thinkers stumbled into—but he deserves credit for making the first great attempt to explain overall how the world and the cosmos work.

Born in 384 B.C. in Stagira, near Macedonia on the north coast of the Aegean Sea, Aristotle [AR-is-TAHTL] became a tutor of Alexander the Great in Macedonia and a student of Plato (born in Athens about 427 B.C.). As a star scholar at Plato's Academy in Athens, he had received the rich legacy of Platonic thought, which built upon the teachings of Plato's teacher, Socrates. But Plato and his students focused on moral and ethical philosophy, stressing the importance of harmony, in particular a kind of

Aristotle, the most famous and the most influential of all ancient Greek thinkers (The Bettmann Archive)

mathematical harmony. To Plato, seeing was not believing; the primary reality, he thought, lay in the realms of mathematics, forms and ideas, rather than purely sensory experiences. And on this point Aristotle challenged his teacher.

To Aristotle, observation—not the abstraction of mathematics—was the best tool for understanding reality. (As it has turned out, both Plato and Aristotle were partly right: Both observation and mathematics have proved important tools in the development of science.) Aristotle believed that whatever divine presence existed in the universe must be a kind of pure intellect. The greatest occupation for humankind was the use of the mind, and the search for natural causes, he thought, was the best thing anyone could do, using objective observation as a tool. But, for all that, Aristotle built the great edifice of his world model not so much on observation as on an intellectual search for an answer to the question, "Why is it all here?" He began by assuming that everything had a purpose, as if controlled by a master plan, and that everything functioned in a way that served its predetermined end purpose. Known as teleology, this major avenue of Aristotle's philosophy unfortunately proved to be a blind alley down which scientists traveled for centuries to come.

In the areas of botany and biology Aristotle made many accurate observations (he was the first to classify dolphins as mammals, for example), as well as some wrong guesses (he believed that the heart was the location of human intellectual activities and the brain merely an organ to cool the blood). Of more direct importance to those who would follow him, though, were Aristotle's ideas about a hierarchy or a kind of "ladder" of life in which all creatures from worms to humans had a specific place. Humans, according to Aristotle, were at the top of this ladder, with all other life forms ranked below in descending order of perfection. Aristotle's ladder was an unbroken continuum in which all possible life forms were represented, but he did not imagine that they evolved in any way or that they ever had.

Some of Aristotle's most enduring thoughts lay in the areas of cosmology and physics. The stars and planets, according to Aristotle, were carried by spheres that rotated around the Earth, a spherical ball in the center of the universe. It was not a new idea; Eudoxus, another student of Plato's, first put it forth to explain the movements of the stars and planets, an enormously puzzling question to the ancients. Once the Greeks began to rationalize all observations—without recourse to spiritual or magical explanations—then the movements seen in the skies posed big problems. Plato had challenged his students to find what orderly system might explain the movements of these objects about the Earth and "save the phenomena" (that is, reconcile theory with observations). Looking at the skies from the Earth and assuming that the Sun, Moon, planets and stars all circled around the Earth, observers saw many puzzles. Why was the path of the Sun irregular? Why did the Moon have a monthly cycle of phases? Why did the planets seem to move east to west and then sometimes seem to move in the opposite direction (a phenomenon known as "retrograde motion")? Eudoxus was the first to come up with a system that seemed to work—almost. The stars, he said, could be thought of as hanging on the inside surface of a huge, dark outer spherical shell. This shell rotated once a day around the Earth east to west on an axis running north to south. Inside it moved the planets, fixed in transparent shells, or spheres—four for each planet. These rotated on different axes and at different, though constant, speeds. Through careful calculations, Eudoxus developed a complex system of more than two dozen such spheres to explain the observed phenomena, such as the cyclical movements of the stars, the daily paths of the Sun and the Moon, the monthly cycle of the Moon, and periodic eclipses. But to Eudoxus, these spheres were a kind of abstract mathematical construct, conceived as part of Plato's world view of harmony, his belief that life and everything in the universe was a sort of unending circle.

Aristotle solidified this idea of a finite universe built of nested, rotating spheres that he believed contained all matter. But he was dissatisfied with the model because it did not explain causes. So he conceived of these concentric spheres, not as just a mathematical explanation, but as a real machine, with spheres made of a transparent material, a sort of crystal-like substance that he called ether. The planets were made of masses of glowing ether. And, because he believed that "nature abhors a vacuum," he thought that all areas between the spheres were also filled with a vapor of ether. To the outer sphere, containing the stars, he assigned the function of "prime mover" of all the other spheres. To explain the irregularity of the planets' paths, he proposed that there must be extra spheres to regulate the planets' motions, located between the planetary spheres of Eudoxus, some moving in the opposite direction from the rest and at different speeds. The entire system, with the spheres for Sun, Moon and stars, now included a total of 55 spheres. Aristotle had found himself in a spot and the only way he saw to save the integrity of his system was to make a complex explanation even more complex, thereby violating one of the first rules of good science as we now know it: Choose the simplest explanation that will work. But it was the best he could come up with, and Aristotle's vision of spheres nested inside spheres persisted well into the Middle Ages as central to the medieval view of the universe.

Aristotle also believed that in the heavenly cosmos all was imperishable with no beginning and no end—everlasting, peaceful and perfect (since little if any change was ever observed there)—whereas on Earth everything was changeable and corrupt. In the heavens, all motion was circular, and thereby harmonious and perfect; on Earth movement could be linear and violent. The heavens, therefore, must have different properties from the Earth, and movement in the cosmos must be governed by different laws.

On Earth, he explained, all substance was divided into four different elements: earth, fire, water and air. Each of these elements moved in such a way as to return to its natural state—explaining why objects drop to the Earth, water "finds its own level," air spreads out into space around it and flames leap upward. He also thought that all elements could be transmuted, or changed, into each other; this theory later provided the philosophical justification for alchemy, the medieval "science" of turning other materials into gold.

Again, most of these explanations seemed to work well together, but there was one major flaw in this scheme of things that Aristotle didn't ever explain satisfactorily: projectile motion. If you didn't push it, a stone would remain at rest or it would move toward the center of the Earth. But what about the movement of a stone that you throw or sling with a slingshot? Why, if all things tend to return to their natural state, will the thrown stone travel horizontally for a distance before dropping to Earth? Aristotle did a sort of patch job on his theory by saying that the air disturbed by the projectile provides a horizontal push once it leaves the force that set it in motion. Even Aristotle was probably not entirely happy with this explanation, but it was the best he could find that would fit in with the rest of his conceptualization. This problem, sometimes referred to as "the arrow problem" or the "projectile problem," is a good example of how one small piece that doesn't fit can be a symptom of bigger flaws in what otherwise may seem to be a good explanation of how things work. But no one would think of a way to solve this problem until the time of Galileo, some 1,900 years later.

FROM ARISTOTLE TO THE HIGH MIDDLE AGES (322 B.C.–A.D. 1449)

With Aristotle Greek philosophy reached its peak. After the death in 323 B.C. of his most famous pupil, Alexander the Great (who had attempted to conquer the same world physically that Aristotle had striven to conquer intellectually), the great days of ancient Greece were over. In Alexander's march of conquest, however, he had spread the best of Greek culture throughout what we now call the Hellenic World, founding in the process the famous city of Alexandria in Egypt. It was there that Greek thought saw its final flowering, facilitated by the magnificent Library of Alexandria until its destruction in 48 B.C. Greek geometry reached its pinnacle with the brilliant work of Euclid (c. 325–c. 270 B.C.) and Apollonius of Perga (c. 262–c. 190 B.C.). And, although few attempts were made at the same kind of ambitious and all-encompassing understanding of nature that Aristotle had presented to the world, the work begun in classic Greece continued in more specialized areas.

With the ancient Greeks, the wheels moving toward modern science had been set in motion.

ARISTARCHUS OF SAMOS, HIPPARCHUS AND PTOLEMY

In the area of astronomy, Aristarchus of Samos (c. 310–c. 230 B.C.) and Hipparchus (c. 190–c. 120 B.C.) continued Aristotle's quest into the nature of the cosmos. With the work of Ptolemy (A.D. c. 100–c. 170) that quest would see the development of a system that, although incorrect, would last throughout the Middle Ages until the Renaissance and the scientific revolution in the 16th and 17th centuries.

Although little of Aristarchus's work survives today and still less is known of his personal life, we do know that he was a brilliant mathematician who was born in Samos and died in Alexandria around 230 B.C. He spent a great deal of time studying the heavens and postulated that the Sun was a great ball of fire, about 20 times larger than the Moon and about 20 times farther away from the Earth. His measurements were much too small, but his reasoning was so exact that scientists today believe that had he had the

---

ASTROLOGY

The practice of astrology began more than 3,000 years ago in ancient Babylonia. It started at a time when most people believed that the planets in the heavens were, variously, themselves gods, or the homes of gods, or representative of the personalities of the gods. People believed that by studying the movements of the planets and how they apparently interacted with one another, they could predict the influences of the gods on the human world. At first they believed that these influences extended only to kings and kingdoms. With the Greeks, though, and their much more humanlike gods, astrologers began to believe that astrology could also predict the influence of the planets and gods on the average human. Needless to say, with this extension of astrology to the average human being, it became much more popular and was practiced by such important Greek thinkers as Hipparchus and Ptolemy. In fact much of the great Greek achievement in the study of the heavens and the movements of the planets was done in an attempt to identify heavenly bodies more correctly and understand their movements for the purposes of making astrological predictions.

Astrology fell into a decline during the Middle Ages, primarily because it was opposed by the Christian church. But it was never completely stifled, and by the time of the Renaissance and the Reformation it had again become very popular, and many scholars and universities endorsed it. With the coming of the scientific revolution, however, the discoveries by such great thinkers as Kepler and Newton showed that the heavens were not a special domain but operated under the same physical laws that operated on Earth. From that time on most scientists and educated people began to turn away from astrology.

Nonetheless, today astrology is still a popular superstition believed in by many people.

Hipparchus at work observatory in Alexandria (Louis Figuier: *Vies des savants illustres depuis l'antiquité jusqu'au dix-neuvième siècle*, vol. II, 1866)

opportunity to work with today's modern instruments he would have come up with a much more correct answer. A man born in the wrong time in many ways, Aristarchus [ar-is-TAHR-kus] also came to the conclusion that Aristotle was incorrect—that the Sun and stars did not revolve around the Earth but that the Earth, Moon and planets revolved around the Sun. It was an inspired observation, but unfortunately he never found a way to prove his guess and it flew in the face of most people's common-sense feeling that if the Earth did actually move they should be able to notice the movements.

Hipparchus [hi-PAHR-kus], often called the greatest of the Greek astronomers, retained the Aristotelian view that the Earth and not the Sun was the center of the universe. Working from his observations made in Turkey and on the island of Rhodes, he made many important observations of the stars and compiled one of the earliest accurate stellar catalogs. More important for the history of science was Hipparchus's attempt to explain why what he saw when he observed the skies did not tally with Aristotle's belief that the celestial bodies moved around the Earth in perfect circles. For instance, if the planets traveled in the same simple kind of path as the Sun, why did they appear to wander erratically across the sky? The word *planet* was, after all, the Greek word for "wanderer." As a solution Hipparchus proposed that the Sun and Moon traveled in circular orbits eccentric to the Earth, that is, they did not move around the Earth's center. And the planets, he proposed, actually made small looplike movements as

Ptolemy, depicted here in his observatory, elaborated on Aristotle's concept of the universe in the second century A.D., and this Ptolemaic system was accepted worldwide for centuries.
(Figuier: *Vies des savants*, vol. II, 1866)

they traveled in the bigger circle on their journey around the Earth. These small circles superimposed upon the larger ones he called epicycles. It was an idea that, once taken up by Ptolemy two centuries later, dominated astronomical thought for many centuries.

If Hipparchus was the greatest of the Greek astronomers, it was Ptolemy [TOL-uh-mee] who, by incorporating many of Hipparchus's concepts and synthesizing the ideas of many others, gave his name to the system that would last until Copernicus would overturn it in 1543. Born Claudius Ptolemaeus about A.D. 100, Ptolemy was probably born in Egypt and may have been either Greek or Egyptian—no one really knows. (But he wasn't a member of the Egyptian royal family of Ptolemies that reigned up to the time just preceding his birth.) He presented his picture of the universe in his book known today as the *Almagest*, in which he summed up most of the results of ancient Greek thinking about the movements of the heavens. The Earth according to Ptolemy was a sphere located at the center of the universe. The known planets, as well as the Moon and Sun, in order of increasing distance from the Earth—the Moon, Venus, Mercury, the Sun, Mars, Jupiter and Saturn—all traveled in a combination of eccentric circles and epicycles around the Earth. Unlike Aristotle, Ptolemy appears to have thought of the spheres that carried the planets not as real objects, but simply as a convenient mathematical and visual representation. If Ptolemy had thought of the spheres as real objects then he would have had to come up with some fancy thinking to explain how his smaller "loops" could interact with them. However, many who did accept the Ptolemaic system *did* continue to think of Aristotle's spheres as being actual objects, while also accepting the Hipparchus-Ptolemaic idea of epicycles. Needless to say, some kind of clarification and clear thinking was sorely wanted, but despite its obvious weaknesses the Ptolemaic system became the standard view of the world for several centuries.

Why, when others such as Aristarchus had proposed alternative views of the universe, did those of Aristotle and Ptolemy win almost total acceptance and hold sway over so many minds for so long? To understand this, it's important to remember that with his carefully reasoned system Aristotle had explained just about all the mysteries of nature to the satisfaction of the ancient Greeks. And, more important, his system offered what might be considered a good "common sense" explanation based on simple and obvious observation for most of its answers. Everyone could see the stone fall, the smoke rise, the Sun and stars circle the Earth. His teleology satisfied the human need to find purpose and meaning in the universe, and his perfect heavens and spheres offered a kind of harmonic beauty above the imperfections of the everyday earthly world.

Most of the problems, at least for the astronomers, came when they tried to make accurate observations and predictions of the heavenly movements based on Aristotle's teachings. Things just didn't always appear to work right. It was this problem that Ptolemy had addressed. How could one retain the spirit of the Aristotelian system and still arrive at more accurate predictions of the planetary movements? The *Almagest* was heavily mathematical and Ptolemy's careful calculations took most of the phenomena into account. It corrected many problems and offered a more useful device from which the astronomers and astrologers could work.

As it stood, Ptolemy's work was just about the last major word on the mysteries of the heavens for nearly 14 centuries. By the time of his death the magnificent era of classical Hellenistic culture was long since over. The Roman era, which had begun with the reign of Augustus Caesar in 27 B.C., was for a long time one of aggressive prosperity, but the Roman mind was more tuned in to such practical matters as engineering, finance and government than the pursuit of science. With the fall of Rome in the 5th century, a long decline of western civilization and spirit followed, during which progress in the natural sciences went into a lengthy stagnation. Not everything was lost, though. Despite the destruction of the magnificent library at Alexandria, much of the writing of Aristotle, as well as other works from the Greco-Roman period, was preserved, most notably by Arab scholars. And, as civilization began slowly to rebuild itself during the Middle Ages, from about 500 to 1500, the teachings of Aristotle, Ptolemy and others of the ancients began to reemerge.

ARCHIMEDES

Archimedes was one of the earliest known scientists to test his hypotheses with experiments.
(Smithsonian Photo # 67,478)

Perhaps the greatest "working scientist" and mathematician of antiquity, Archimedes [ahr-kih-MEE-deez] was born around 287 B.C., a native of Syracuse, Sicily. Archimedes made many original contributions to geometry but unlike many other of the ancients he was also a practical, hands-on thinker, and he turned his mind and ingenuity to many problems of both a scientific and engineering nature.

Besides such mathematical achievements as calculating the value of pi (the ratio of the length of the circumference of a circle to its diameter) better than any other mathematician in the ancient world, he also loved mechanical

THE SCHOLASTIC ERA

This reemergence did not come easily. In the long struggle of the Christian church to hold the western world together during its centuries of turmoil, the church had gained much power and control over the minds of most western thinkers. And, although there was much in the Aristotelian philos-

devices. He is reported to have invented or perfected many war machines, including the catapult and, according to legend, a specially constructed mirror which he used to turn the rays of the Sun upon enemy warships in the harbor of Syracuse, burning their sails in the process.

He was the first to give a systematic account of the determinations of the center of gravity, working out in full detail the principle of the lever. "Give me a place to stand on and I can move the world," he is reported to have said about his understanding of the lever. And his famous run through the streets of Syracuse in the nude while crying "Eureka!"—meaning, "I've got it!"—supposedly came about after he discovered, while taking a bath, his principle that submerged bodies displace their own volume of liquid and have their weight diminished by an amount equal to the weight of the liquid displaced.

While the famous Archimedes' screw, a hollow, helical cylinder that pumped water upward when rotated, was probably borrowed by him from the ancient Egyptians, there is little doubt that his was one of the finest scientific and engineering minds of the ancient Greco-Roman world.

Famous even in his own time, Archimedes was killed in 212 B.C. during the Roman sack of Syracuse. According to the legend, the Roman general in charge had given his soldiers orders that when found, Archimedes was to be unharmed and treated with respect. Archimedes was discovered while engaged in drawing a geometrical diagram in the sand, the city burning around him. He reportedly waved a Roman soldier impatiently away while he returned to his problem. The equally impatient Roman drew his sword and ended Archimedes' life. Hearing of this act representing so clearly the stupidity of war, the Romans in command sadly gave Archimedes an honorable and official burial.

Combining the mathematical emphasis of Plato with the physical reasoning of Aristotle, Archimedes might have gone on to make even greater contributions to humanity's understanding of the laws of nature. His impact might have equalled Galileo's nearly 2,000 years later.

ophy that fitted well with official church doctrine, there were also many points that dramatically and uncomfortably diverged from it. Averroës [uh-VER-oh-eez] (1126–1198), the Spanish-Arab philosopher—and the most important scholar of Aristotelian thought in Islam—taught that both religion and natural philosophy were important ways to seek the truth, but he doubted that the two could ever be merged comfortably into a single system.

By the middle of the 13th century, though, Aristotelian ideas had become so firmly established within the Christian universities that Thomas Aquinas [uh-KWY-nus] (c. 1225–1274), disturbed by the discrepancies between Aristotle and the official teaching of the church, attempted to unite both into a single comprehensive system. With much hard work and editing of Aristotle, Aquinas offered a solution. Although disturbing to some of the more purist Aristotelian scholars, his ideas managed to satisfy most church officials enough to become the church's official doctrine. Under Aquinas's interpretation, for instance, Aristotle's "Prime Mover" could be viewed as "God." The heavens were perfect and harmonious, and the movement of the Aristotelian spheres could be seen as being accomplished by the will power of angels. For much (but not all) of Christendom the Earth by the Middle Ages was again seen not as spherical but as flat, and its creation was envisioned exactly as described in the Bible.

ISLAMIC SCIENTISTS AND THE ARISTOTELIAN TRADITION

Arab scientists such as Averroës played a key part in the development of world science during the Middle Ages, not only through their own contributions, but also as preservers and transmitters of knowledge. In centers as far-flung as Baghdad and Damascus in the Middle East, Cairo in Egypt, and Córdoba in Spain, the Arabs had enthusiastically adopted the Greek scientific tradition and preserved the writings of Aristotle, his colleagues and disciples, and many other Greek thinkers. And in the 12th and 13th centuries, many works of Greek science came into the hands of Western European thinkers during contacts between Muslims and Christians in Spain and Sicily and were then translated from Arabic into Latin (the universal scholarly language in Europe at the time). While the most important and influential translations of Aristotle were made directly from the Greek into Latin, the Arabs made a signal contribution in preserving many writings that had otherwise been lost during the destructive invasions by barbarians in Western Europe and Alexandria.

Arab scientists also, no doubt, contributed to the great adulation of Aristotle in medieval Europe, seeing his ideas as the foundation of all knowledge about the natural world. In the words of Averroës, Aristotle "comprehended the whole truth—by which I mean that quantity which human nature, insofar as it is human, is capable of grasping." It was an idea shared and echoed long and loud by the medieval scholastics in monasteries and institutions of learning throughout Europe.

It wasn't only the works of Aristotle and Ptolemy that became so dogmatically enshrined during the Middle Ages. In the fields of the life sciences the work of Galen (A.D. c. 130–c. 200) in medicine and of Dioscorides [dee-os-KOR-uh-deez] around A.D. 50 and Pliny [PLIH-nee] (A.D. 23–79) also became standard and dogmatically revered references.

Galen [GAY-len], the most famous Greek physician after Hippocrates, practiced his profession in Rome under the reign of Marcus Aurelius and his successors. Even though he was allowed to perform his dissections only on pigs and other animals, he wrote extensively about human anatomy. He identified many muscles for the first time and also was one of the first to demonstrate the importance of the spinal cord. Much of Galen's voluminous work survived and, although in error much of the time, like Aristotle's, became a revered and unquestioned authority to those struggling to relight the lamps of human knowledge.

Dioscorides, a Greek physician who preceded Galen, wrote the first pharmacopoeia (a catalog of useful drugs and their preparation), *De materia medica*, which survived to the Middle Ages. And Pliny, known as Pliny the Elder to distinguish him from his nephew, the Roman orator, composed a 37-volume catalog of the wonders of nature and animals, entitled *Naturalis Historia*. Usually known today simply as Pliny's *Natural History*, the work contained many useful descriptions as well as many absurdly simplistic errors. Like the work of Aristotle, Dioscorides and Galen, it, too, became enshrined in the scholastic era of the Middle Ages as the final word on the subject—the unquestioned wisdom of the ancients.

It's easy today to look back in frustration at much of the thinking that was done (or not done) by the "scholastics" of the latter part of the Middle Ages. A lot of it looks pretty silly, and even looked foolish to some of its critics at the time. Many hours were spent poring over and interpreting the books of the ancient Greeks rather than seeking answers directly from nature itself. One critic, for instance, complained that his scholastic contemporaries would argue for days about how many teeth a horse had, pulling out ancient authority after ancient authority, when all they had to do was go out and open a horse's mouth. But it's important to remember that original thinking in natural philosophy had been almost totally absent between the end of the Greco-Roman era in the 6th century and the scholastic era from the 10th to the 15th century. In this new, emerging world, dominated by the Christian church and its uncomfortable relationship with what today we call science, many barriers existed in the minds of people about the best way to study what was considered "God's world." And most of the scholastics themselves, it must be remembered were just that, scholars, men of books and letters, who saw their jobs as preserving—comprehending and keeping alive the thinking of the ancients who had composed those great books. With the Christian universities and the official doctrines of the church in control of most teaching and scholarly thought, it was difficult for those practicing other professions—astronomers, physicians, and so on, to escape being tied to the beliefs of the ancient past, especially when so many of those beliefs had been welded to the official doctrine of the powerful Christian church.

Thus, while some (men like Roger Bacon, Jean Buridan, William of Ockham, Nicolas of Cusa, and others about whom you will hear more later in this book) objected to and questioned the final authority of the ancient Greeks, for the most part thinkers of the Middle Ages found comfort in believing simply in the world they had inherited. After the years of barbarous darkness that befell the Western world following the fall of Rome, the lights, it seemed to them, were still capable of burning. The thoughts of the great Greeks had survived. And that, in itself, must have seemed some kind of miracle. Who then was to question what must have been so perfectly pre-ordained? For the thinkers of that time, it was enough to worship at the feet of the Greek giants. It would be for others later to climb instead to their shoulders and see the world with much clearer eyes.

SCIENCE IN INDIA AND CHINA

The early development of science was by no means confined to the few communities scattered around the shores of the Mediterranean. Other cultures, meanwhile, had also achieved major developments in technology and science, some of which flowed into the pot of intellectual tools, ideas and theories that ultimately produced the scientific revolution in Western Europe. A prime example is the system of so-called Arabic numerals, originally developed by the Hindus in India, based on a decimal system used as far back as the Vedic period, the earliest in Hindu history, around 1500 B.C. The abstract Hindu numeric system was passed on to medieval Europe by Arab scholars, who had already put the system to use.

Hindu scholars also excelled in the study of language, its structure and its development, and linguistics became to Hindu science what mathematics and geometry were to Greek science: a wellspring of logical thought and exploration. The Hindus also explored areas of mathematics, such as algebra, with success. And they developed extensive systems of knowledge and theory in health care and medicine. They saw the human body as a blend of the five elements (very similar to the Greek elements) of ether, air, fire, water and earth, and the human being as the conscious witness within. Health problems were caused when the elements air, fire and water (renamed wind, bile and phlegm) got out of balance in the body. The Hindus developed both herbal and surgical methods as part of the ayurvedic tradition (based on the *Ayurveda*, written about 2,900 years ago), which sought to restore the balance of the elements in the body. They recognized atomism as the basis of matter as early as 2,500 years ago, although they otherwise never showed much interest in physics. Most of India's scientific developments, however, remained isolated on that subcontinent and did not much affect the development of science in the rest of the world.

China made prodigious early achievements in science and, especially, in technology—often far before similar breakthroughs were achieved in the West. But, with a few exceptions, because of its geographic isolation (great mountain ranges by land and virtually impassable seas acting as barriers), most inventions and discoveries made by the Chinese did not mingle with Western thinking until after the scientific revolution in Western Europe.

Most scholars attribute to the Chinese the invention of paper, gunpowder and the magnetic compass and the development of silk, all of which were imported to the West. They made countless other technological and agricultural advances, excelling as well in several areas of science, developing finely honed skills in observation, logic, mathematics, and organization and collection of data.

For example, the Chinese made superior astronomical observations, both early and often. Chinese astronomers regularly observed and recorded novas and supernovas (sudden brightening—hence *nova*, "new"—of stars in the night sky caused by explosions that produce huge quantities of bright, glowing gas), including the supernovas of 1006, 1054, 1572 and 1604. Most of these were completely ignored or missed by European astronomers, who were so attached to the Aristotelian idea that the heavens were perfect that, for example, no record at all outside China and Japan exists of the great supernova of 1054. The Chinese also were the first to systematically catalog the stars in the skies. And Chinese geographers made some of the earliest accurate maps, their tradition of scientific mapmaking greatly preceding that in the West, where religious beliefs tended to inhibit accurate representations. As early as A.D. 100, Chang Heng (Zhang Heng) introduced a grid system for mapmaking that greatly improved accuracy. Weather records, though rough, date back as far as 1216 B.C. in China, and by the 12th century A.D., the Chinese geologist Chu Hsi (Zhu Xi) had established that mountains were elevated land masses that had once formed the sea floor—a fact not recognized in the West until the 19th century.

But not until after the 17th century, when navigational advances broke through the isolation, could the rest of the world profit from Chinese scientific development. From that time on, both traditions would finally become merged into a world science. Before that time, however, for reasons that are unclear, China did not undergo a process similar to Europe's scientific revolution. Perhaps the great shake-up of world views that became the Renaissance, the Reformation and the birth of modern science in Western Europe required the precise mix of factors that happened to occur first in Italy, and later in France, the rest of Western Europe and England between the 14th and the 17th centuries. In any case, what happened there during that time would come to change forever the way people looked at the world and explored the way it works.

THE PHYSICAL SCIENCES

THE UNIVERSE TURNED OUTSIDE-IN: COPERNICUS, TYCHO AND KEPLER

In the middle of all sits Sun enthroned.

—Nicolaus Copernicus

The last years of the 1400s and the early years of the 1500s were an exciting time to be a student. Explorers and adventurers were roaming the known and unknown world and sending tales back home. Artists, writers and philosophers were busy. This was the time of such multi-talented giants as Leonardo da Vinci (1452–1519) and Michelangelo (1475–1564). Students in the streets and taverns talked about the glories of the ancient, classical past and, freed from the stagnant philosophies of the medieval period, they had begun to look with excitement toward the future.

New worlds lay on the horizon, and new realms of inquiry loomed ahead. It now seemed that after a long sleep the world was awakening to a bright future. As scientists like to say, all the paradigms seemed to be shifting. That is, people's systems of interlocking facts and theories—which once had seemed so reasonable and certain—now seemed as unstable as sand dunes.

This was the bustling world that Nicolaus Copernicus entered in 1491 when he began his student days at the University of Krakow in Poland. In the year before Columbus's famous voyage, Copernicus was on a voyage of his own, into the new world of knowledge and intellectual discovery that was for him as engrossing as the life of any sea captain charting unknown shores.

COPERNICUS AND THE BIRTH OF A REVOLUTION

Niklas Koppernigk was born February 19, 1473 in the town of Torun, a commercial center in what is now north-central Poland. His father was a wholesale copper dealer (from which the family may have taken its name) from Krakow, and his mother, Barbara Waczenrode, came from a respected local German family. By the time Niklas, the youngest of four children, reached the age of 10, both his parents had died, and his 36-year-old uncle, Lucas Waczenrode, became guardian of the orphaned children. While the death of his parents must have been a profound personal tragedy to young Niklas, the shift of guardianship to his uncle was of tremendous consequence. It's difficult to know what kind of life Niklas might have followed if his parents had survived. Following the customs of the time, he probably would have followed his father into the commercial trade. But under the guardianship of his uncle an entirely different world of opportunities opened up.

Nicolaus Copernicus
(Mary Lea Shane Archives
of Lick Observatory)

34

Lucas Waczenrode, a scholar who had studied at Krakow, Leipzig and Prague and received a doctorate of canon law with high honors from the University of Bologna, had become bishop of Ermland (or Varmia), a small principality on the Baltic Sea, in 1489. Understanding the importance of learning and having enough financial resources and social prestige to aid his charges, Waczenrode encouraged Niklas and his brother Andreas to enter the University of Krakow, which they both did two years after their uncle became bishop. By the time Niklas was 22, his uncle had secured for him a lifetime appointment as a canon at Frauenburg Cathedral. The position meant a good income for Niklas for the rest of his life. And although there were duties that needed to be attended to, the post did not call for his continual presence, and through successive leaves of absence he was able to continue his academic studies for nearly a dozen years more. At some point during his student days Niklas Koppernigk latinized his name to Nicolaus Copernicus [ko-PUR-nuh-kus]—a ritual common among students of his time, a way of announcing their respect for the classic past and their intellectual fraternity with one another.

Nicolaus Copernicus was an intellectually restless young man with a talent for ideas, and during the flowering of the Renaissance he had the perfect opportunity to pursue them. He quickly fit into university life, avidly buying books (a new and wonderful possibility since the invention of the printing press) and attending lectures in the fine school of mathematics and astronomy. He explored the humanist ideas from Italy that had begun to gain strength against the more rigid tenets of scholasticism at Krakow. Drawn by the bright, intellectually creative light of Italy, by 1496 Copernicus moved on to the University of Bologna, and he later studied at Padua and Ferrara. In Italy he entered deeper into the world of the scholarly humanists, a world that saw students traveling from university to university and writing long, elegant letters on philosophy, art and life. These letters were often distributed like pamphlets and eagerly read by their fellow students. And young Copernicus was one of them, an intellectual nomad, devouring knowledge in this swarming, restless center of humanism. He studied canon law and pursued his first loves, astronomy and mathematics, as well as Greek, medicine, philosophy and Roman law. In Bologna he had a chance to study with Domenico Maria da Novara (1454–1504), one of the greatest astronomers of the day. Not just a student, Copernicus apparently also served as an assistant, probably rooming in his professor's home. These student days laid the foundation for the great role that Copernicus would play in the scientific revolution.

Although Copernicus studied both canon law and medicine, as far back as his days at the University of Krakow, his first love was astronomy. He read all the books he could find on the subject and took every opportunity he had to learn about observation as it was practiced in his time. In Bologna, under the guidance of his mentor Novara, he made his first recorded astronomical observation.

A critical reader and thinker, Copernicus's astronomical studies quickly led him to become bothered by many inconsistencies in the Ptolemaic (geocentric, or earth-centered) model of the universe. As some astronomers had begun to point out, Ptolemy's system made just too many predictions that didn't correspond with their actual observations. They were frequently off by many hours or even days. Many people had begun to suspect that something had to be wrong with this complex and unwieldy system of spheres and epicycles.

Moreover, a great revival of Platonism, with its emphasis on mathematics, simplicity and perfection, coursed through southern Europe at the time, and Novara, Copernicus's astronomy teacher, was among those at its helm. A lover of Platonic simplicity and mathematical beauty couldn't find much harmony or gracefulness in Ptolemy's awkward and complicated system. Copernicus apparently began very early to consider another, simpler idea about the structure of the universe: a heliocentric system, with the Sun at the center and orbited by the Earth and planets.

Of course, he was not the first to do so. Several of the ancient Greeks had put forth similar ideas, including Pythagoras and Aristarchus of Samos. But Ptolemy's complex system, with the Earth at the center, had been accepted and taught as fact for more than 1,300 thousand years. The Ptolemaic system also fit well with Christian theology, which saw humans as the centerpiece of creation, made in the image of God. It was only right that the Earth then, the home to humans, should hold such a favored place. And it seemed intuitively correct to anyone viewing the night sky and watching the way all the celestial objects seemed to pass overhead.

In 1503 Copernicus finished his doctorate in canon law and returned to Frauenburg to take up his administrative duties there. He had barely settled in, however, when his uncle became ill in Heilsberg and called him to his side as his personal physician. Three years later Copernicus relocated to Heilsberg and remained there with his uncle from 1506 to 1512, when the bishop died. It was probably during this time that he set down his first rough drafts about the heliocentric universe.

By 1514, after returning to Frauenburg, he had roughed out a synopsis of his new system that he cautiously passed around among friends. Known as the *Commentariolus* ("Short Commentary"), this work formed the basis for a more thorough presentation, *De revolutionibus orbium coelestium* (*On the Revolutions of the Celestial Spheres*), which he worked on for most of the rest of his life.

From his rooms in a corner tower of the fortress cathedral of Frauenburg, Copernicus could see the skies above the Baltic Sea. He set up a small observatory on the roof and equipped it with a few standard astronomical instruments of the time (the telescope had not yet been invented), and he occasionally climbed to the tower to make his observations.

But, while Copernicus was recognized in his time as an important astronomer, he relied primarily on the observations of others, including Ptolemy, and instead spent his time making precise mathematical calculations and poring over his books. He carefully compared versions of Ptolemy's *Almagest* for possible mistakes in the copying or translations and spent many an evening deep in thought. Like the Greeks that he so much admired, he trusted more in the powers of reason than in observation.

The problem he had inherited from Ptolemy was how to explain the strange behavior of the planets. While the Sun, Moon and stars seemed to circle overhead once every 24 hours in a way that seemed comfortably predictable, the planets did not. Sometimes, as the Greeks had observed, these "wanderers" seemed to double back, in a retrograde motion. For his solution to this problem Ptolemy had explained that each planet moved in small circles around an invisible center which in turn moved in a larger circle orbiting the Earth. Imagine that you are running around a large circle, and every so often you change direction and make a little loop in your run and then continue on your way along the circle again. This basic concept, which he called epicycles, served roughly to reconcile the differences between observation and Aristotle's earlier theory that all heavenly objects rotated around the Earth in concentric spheres, set one within the other. But, as

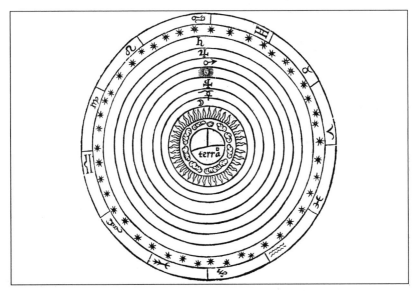

In Ptolemy's system the Earth ("terra") was at the center of the Solar System. The Sun, Moon and all the planets revolved around the Earth. (Courtesy, Owen Gingerich)

more frequent and better observations were made, Ptolemy's system appeared more and more to be failing its observational tests. Some astronomers were desperately beginning to add even more spheres and epicycles to the already complicated Ptolemaic system. Copernicus, however, perhaps longing for a simpler, more mathematically elegant explanation, would later write, "A system of this sort seemed neither sufficiently absolute nor sufficiently pleasing to the mind."

The great medieval scholar William of Ockham (c. 1285–1349), although not a Platonist, had cautioned against adopting such complicated theories when he advised that "entities must not needlessly be multiplied." Many scientists today subscribe to this idea, known as "Ockham's Razor," taking it to mean that, when two theories both seem to fit the observed facts, the theory that requires the fewest assumptions is probably better. To this day, believing that nature's laws are simple (even though nature itself may be complicated), scientists tend to prefer a theory that is simple and neat to one that is complicated and messy.

Copernicus was faced with a messy theory. What he needed was a simpler and neater one.

What, Copernicus asked, would happen to all of the observations and calculations if he redrew the Ptolemaic scheme to have the planets circle the Sun instead of the Earth? He decided to try it. The decision required an entirely different and revolutionary way of looking at the universe.

As he later wrote in *Revolutions*, ". . . I began to meditate upon the mobility of the Earth . . . although the opinion seemed absurd." Still, he thought, as a reasoning human being he should have the freedom, as the Greeks did, to entertain any possible explanation to solve his problems—including the idea that the Earth, not the Sun, was moving. And, although a few Greek philosophers had speculated on that same idea, they had not elaborated on it, or attempted to fit it in with actual observations or calculations. Copernicus, for the first time, not only considered the idea, but attempted to calculate the results of a planetary system with interrelated, circular orbits around the Sun, instead of the Earth. It was a long and difficult job. But in the end he was convinced that his new system was true. The Sun and not the Earth was the center of the planetary orbits.

Why then did they all appear to be revolving around the Earth? The Earth, he maintained, revolves around its own axis once every 24 hours, causing the heavens to appear to move overhead. The Sun's distance from the Earth, he believed, was negligible compared to the great distance of the fixed stars (which he thought hung at the outer edge of space just beyond the last visible planet). The apparent motion of the Sun through an annual cycle is caused by the Earth revolving around the Sun (not vice versa). Only the Moon, he said, revolves around the Earth. And the strange, mysterious retrogressions in the movement of Mars, Jupiter and Saturn (the three outer

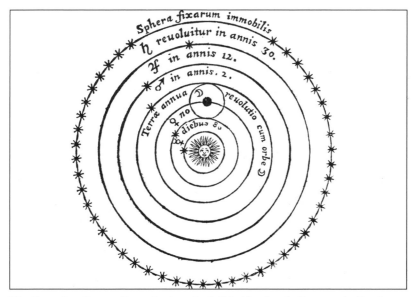

The Copernican System. Copernicus conceived of the idea that the Sun, not the Earth, was at the center of the Solar System (Courtesy, Owen Gingerich)

planets known at the time) are caused by the fact that they, like the Earth, are moving around the Sun—but farther away. The Earth, traveling in a smaller orbit around the Sun, would sometimes pass up these outer planets in their longer orbits, making them look like they were moving backward across the sky.

It all seemed to make sense, Copernicus thought, and had a certain beauty and simplicity, once you allowed yourself to break free from the idea that the Earth must be the center of the universe. But that idea had remained supreme for hundreds of years and had deep roots, not only in religious and secular thought, but in everyone's "common sense": looking up at the sky they saw "the Sun move" while the Earth under their feet obviously stood still. He feared, as he would later write, that "certain people . . . will immediately shout to have me and my opinion hooted off the stage," further explaining:

> *I hesitated for a long time as to whether I should publish that which I have written to demonstrate the earth's motion, or whether it would not be better to follow the example of the Pythagoreans, who used to hand down the secrets of philosophy to their relatives and friends in oral form. . . . I was almost impelled to put the finished work wholly aside, through the scorn I had reason to anticipate on account of the newness and apparent contrariness to reason of my theory.*

In 1539, a young German Lutheran professor of mathematics arrived in Frauenburg to seek out the renowned astronomer. His latinized name was

Rheticus (born Georg Joachim von Lauchen), and he had long admired Copernicus, having heard with interest about the canon's ideas on a heliocentric system, which had privately circulated years before in the *Commentariolus*. And, although Copernicus remained reluctant, the younger man finally talked him into going public. And so, the first publication on the Copernican system was a summary written by Rheticus that appeared in 1540. Many people assume that Copernicus had held back his ideas "almost four times nine years," as he put it, because he feared retribution from the Catholic church. But if he expected an official outcry as a result of this venture made by Rheticus, he must have been relieved now. On the contrary, both the pope and a cardinal of the church numbered among those who encouraged him to publish the full manuscript. (Those who would follow would not be so lucky, for Copernicus lived just at the end of a period of relative tolerance in the Catholic church, a time when the church seemed to see little conflict between science and Christian dogma.)

Rheticus, bold, aspiring and industrious, set to work supervising the publication. But the final stages of printing were overseen by Andreas Osiander, a leading Lutheran theologian in Nuremberg, who, for unclear reasons, wrote and added an unsigned preface, without Copernicus's approval. Osiander may have hoped to appease Martin Luther, founder of the Lutheran church, who had already gone on record against Copernicus, declaring that "this fool wishes to reverse the entire science of astronomy; but sacred Scripture tells us that Joshua commanded the Sun to stand still, and not the Earth." Osiander's preface specified that the Copernican system was purely hypothetical, an imaginative way to help astronomers predict the positions of the planets but not necessarily one that was intended to represent reality. Even slow as he had been to publish, the cautious Copernicus would probably never have approved this sidestep from the truth. But the first copies, according to legend, arrived from the printer on the day Copernicus died, and we may never know for certain if he even saw the controversial preface.

TYCHO BRAHE, OBSERVER OF THE STARS

In 1543, the Copernican system had simplicity, regularity and consistency going for it, and it did make better astronomical predictions, at least some of the time. But, actually, that was about all—at the time. Aside from this slight edge, either Ptolemy's geocentric theory or Copernicus's heliocentric theory might have been true for all anyone knew. Both explained why the planets sometimes seemed to move backward—"saved the phenomena" as the Greeks liked to say. No one had proof either way, no observations that

Tycho Brahe (Mary
Lea Shane Archives of
Lick Observatory)

confirmed either point of view more than the other. Each was just a theory. The Copernican system's qualities of simplicity, regularity and consistency were satisfying in a way, but one can't decide that something is true based on this kind of satisfaction alone. At least, that's not a scientific approach. In science, elegance and reasonableness are not the same as experimental proof. Proof can only come from thinking about what observation or experiment might prove the point; then observing, repeating, and observing again; and, finally, looking at the results. In the 16th century, if you wanted to find out the truth about how the universe worked, you had to look at the skies—at the Moon, the planets and the stars—and you had to look long and carefully.

The greatest astronomical observer before the invention of the telescope was a strange and colorful individual named Tycho Brahe [ty-ko BRAH-uh] (1546–1601), who was born three years after the death of Copernicus. The son of a Danish nobleman, he became known as Tycho, a latinization of his Danish given name, Tyge. At 13, evidently something of a child prodigy, he entered the University of Copenhagen. He was initially intent on entering politics, but in 1560, at age 14, Tycho Brahe suddenly changed his mind forever when he saw an eclipse of the Sun. From that time on, Tycho

41

would pursue the path of skywatcher with an unprecedented avidity, precision and concern for documentation.

Tycho Brahe had a big belly, an unpleasant sense of his own elevated station, and a fiery temper. At age 18 he got into a duel with another mathematician over an obscure mathematical point and his opponent sliced off part of Tycho's nose with his sword; Tycho replaced it with a prominent bridge of alloy metal (a long-contested point of legend that was recently confirmed when his grave was opened and his remains were inspected). Haughty and proud, he is said to have made all his observations in noble dress. He liked living well; he had a well-stocked wine cellar and kept a large group of servants, including a dwarf, to serve and amuse him. It's also said that he owned his own private dungeon in which to incarcerate and punish his servants and the peasants living on his land when they broke one of his many strict rules.

Tycho's foster father had died of pneumonia while saving the life of Danish king Frederick II, and out of gratitude, the king gave Tycho an island off the coast near Copenhagen. He also granted him carte blanche for

Tycho Brahe in his observatory in Denmark (Smithsonian Institution Libraries)

building the ultimate astronomical observatory of his day. By 1580 the observatory was complete, at a cost of some $1.5 million in today's money. With his sharp eyes and great attention to detail, as well as his elaborate, expensive and beautifully crafted precision instruments (many devised by him), Tycho produced far better data than anyone—Ptolemy or Copernicus—had ever had to work with. With utter exactness and painstaking concentration he watched in his observatory hour after hour, night after night, detailing the positions of the stars, recording the times of their appearances and chronicling the positions of the planets.

By the time his observatory was finished, his watchfulness had already been rewarded by two extraordinary events in the nighttime skies. In 1572, Tycho spotted a "new star," or nova. (Sometimes called "Tycho's star," it actually was a faint star that exploded in what we now call a supernova). It was only the third nova to be sighted since the time of Hipparchus; the others, seen in 1006 and 1054 by Japanese and Chinese astronomers, were not well known to the still-isolated European scientific community. To those who still clung to Aristotle's idea that the cosmos beyond the Moon was perfect and unchanging, this new stab of light in the night sky cut deep.

Five years later, in 1577, a comet appeared—another unsettling sight to both astronomers and superstitious people. To this day, scientists are not sure where comets come from; they probably originate in an area known as the Oort Cloud, beyond the edge of the Solar System. They arc through the Solar System toward the Sun, streak closely around it and then speed back out in the direction from which they came. Although comets had appeared before in the skies, Aristotle had explained them (along with meteors) as atmospheric events that took place within the changing realm of the Earth, between the Earth and the Moon. Many people took the appearance of comets as dire warnings of impending earthly disasters (and some people still do). Now, with his superior instruments, Tycho made exacting measurements that proved indisputably that this comet had little to do with the Earth and was following a path deep in the skies well beyond the Moon. Tycho also saw that the comet followed an elliptical path, thereby delivering another blow to the idea of perfection in the heavens, since, according to Aristotle, only the circle was perfect. And another of Aristotle's theories was threatened at the same time: If the heavens were composed of nested, crystalline spheres, how could the comet's path arc through them as Tycho's observations clearly showed it did? Even Copernicus, with his new theory, had still left room for the traditional solid spheres. "Now it is quite clear to me that there are no solid spheres in the heavens," Tycho wrote defiantly. And now, at the end of the 16th century, suddenly much that had been taken for granted was called into question because of sights everyone could see—sights that also were seen and, moreover, measured by a strange, meticulous and cranky skywatcher with a metal nose.

Tycho, however, remained unconvinced that the Earth moved around the Sun as Copernicus had suggested. He agreed with Copernicus that Mars and the other planets orbited the Sun, but, if the Earth moved, he reasoned, we would feel it. This was not an unreasonable assumption in his time. If one crossed a meadow on horseback, one felt the wind rushing by; if one rode in a carriage, one felt the jostle and roll of the wheels. What could he know about movement in a vacuum (which no one at the time believed could exist), or about continuous, unaccelerated movement, without changes in direction? (We come close to experiencing this last type of movement when we ride in an airplane cruising smoothly at more than 500 mph, but this experience was not available to Tycho.) So Tycho, a much better observer than theorist, proposed his own compromise system—a combination of Ptolemy's and Copernicus's—which he revealed in a book on the comet of 1577, published in 1583. Tycho accepted the idea that the planets orbit around the Sun, but he suggested that the Sun itself revolves around the Earth. Thus, Tycho preserved the traditional geocentric universe while preserving Copernicus's compositionally helpful idea that put the Sun at the center of the rest of the planetary system.

But Tycho's luck was about to change for the worse, at least temporarily. His patron, Frederick II, died in 1588 and was succeeded by Christian IV, who didn't share Frederick's gratitude or admiration for the irascible astronomer. By 1597, the king had taken back Tycho's island with its observatory and said farewell to Tycho. As a result, Tycho headed for Germany and the court of Emperor Rudolf II, who invited him to take up new quarters in Prague, where he would serve as imperial mathematician, a sort of glorified astrological soothsayer. It was a time of warring nations and warring religions. Everyone seemed to be killing everyone else, Protestant pitted against Catholic, Catholic against Protestant. The choices open to a traveling astronomer were few, and Tycho gladly accepted, knowing that in his spare time he could continue his observations. By now in his fifties, he also began to look for an assistant to help him analyze his enormously voluminous unpublished data.

In 1599, the last year of the 16th century, he found Johannes Kepler.

JOHANNES KEPLER AND THE ELLIPTICAL ORBIT

Or, more accurately Kepler found Tycho. When Johannes Kepler (1571–1630) encountered Tycho, the younger man had already led a checkered career as a quasi-astronomer and astrologer, often unpaid for his services, unhappily married, the laughing stock of his university cohorts. But he had written a book, published in 1596, that attempted to make Plato's ideas

Johannes Kepler
(Mary Lea Shane Archives
of Lick Observatory)

about solids and spheres in the heavens fit with the new idea of the Copernican system. The book was more mystical than scientific and left many astronomers more mystified than edified, but Kepler's grasp of mathematics attracted Tycho.

The two men did not get along well. Kepler felt that Tycho held back the knowledge that the younger man had come to him seeking. "Tycho did not give me the chance to share his practical knowledge, except in conversation during meals, today something about the apogee, tomorrow something about the nodes of another planet." Several times, Kepler threatened to leave.

Finally, Tycho gave in, with a vengeance. Take Mars, he said, and analyze the observations. Braggart to the core, Kepler announced that he would have the answer in eight days. What he did not know was that the movements of Mars, easily seen in the night sky, had been thoroughly and accurately documented; nor did he know that the movements did not remotely correspond to anyone's expectations. The project took Kepler not eight days, but eight years. When he was finished, he would find the mistakes not only in both the Copernican and Ptolemaic systems, but in Tycho's also.

Fortunately, perhaps, for Tycho, he did not live to see the fruits of Kepler's painstaking work. The colorful and obstinate Tycho died in 1601 of a burst bladder (having drunk too much beer at a royal feast that he felt he could not leave). "Let me not seem to have died in vain," he pleaded on his deathbed. He was succeeded as imperial mathematician by Kepler, who, in essence, answered his plea.

"Tycho," Kepler once said of his mentor's vast bank of data, "was superlatively rich, but he knows not how to make proper use of it as is the case with most rich people." Kepler, now in charge of Tycho's store of data, knew exactly how to make use of it.

Unlike Tycho, Kepler believed that Copernicus had the right idea, and he set out to discover, among the rich resources gathered by Tycho, proof of the general plan of the Solar System, starting with the problems presented by Mars. Observations showed that the planets, including and especially Mars, traveled at variable speeds, now slower, now faster, with the rate increasing the closer they drew to the Sun. For six years Kepler tried out various hypotheses that he thought might explain this weirdness. He tested each one by performing voluminous calculations. Of course, he didn't have a computer to crunch the numbers for him, or even a pocket calculator or a slide rule, so that pursuing these questions took not only a great deal of time, but also concentration and expertise. Finally, reluctantly, he came to the conclusion that the orbits of the planets could not be circular.

He published his results in 1609 in a book called *Astronomia Nova* ("New Astronomy"), in which he set forth the first two of what are known as Kepler's laws of planetary motion. For those who concerned themselves with such questions (not everyone, of course, did), his book was earth-shattering. Kepler proposed, completely contrary to his own Platonic leanings and Christian theology, that the planets traveled not in the mystically perfect circles of the Aristotelian and Ptolemaic systems, but in an elliptical path, a relatively imperfect sort of squashed circle. Instead of having one center, an ellipse has two foci (plural of *focus*), and the Sun, Kepler said, was located at one of the two foci. (This is the substance of Kepler's first law.) This idea alone was sufficiently radical to cause the College of Cardinals to suppress Kepler's book.

In his second law, Kepler set forth a mathematical formula describing a planet's variations in speed during its orbit around the Sun. In sum it said that, as a planet moves around the Sun, an imaginary line from the Sun to the planet would sweep over equal areas in equal periods of time. As a result, the closer the planet came to the Sun, the shorter the imaginary line and the faster the planet would have to move to cover an equal area.

Meanwhile, in 1604, Kepler had sighted the second nova to be seen in less than 40 years, known as "Kepler's star." The event shook the European intellectual community and, along with the other confluences of the Renaissance and Reformation years, contributed to a turbulent atmosphere of new ideas and questioned assumptions. Perhaps, a group of philosophers following in the Epicurean tradition went so far as to propose, a concourse of atoms had by chance fallen together to form the new star. But Platonism, with its emphasis on harmony and the "music of the spheres," still reigned in the hearts of the humanists. And Kepler, still very religious, disputed the hint of a universe ruled by chance with an anecdote about a salad his wife served him one evening at supper:

"It seems then," said I aloud, "that if pewter dishes, leaves of lettuce, grains of salt, drops of water, vinegar and oil, and slices of egg, had been flying about in the air from all eternity, it might at last happen by chance that there would come a salad." "Yes," says my wife, "but not so nice and well dressed as this of mine."

Still greatly influenced by Platonic thought, Kepler now set out to determine the relationship he was sure must exist between the distance of a planet's orbit from the Sun and the time it took for the planet to travel around the Sun. And he succeeded. In 1619 he published his third law in *Harmonices Mundi* (*Harmonies of the World*). The square of any planet's period of revolution about the Sun, he said, is proportional to the cube of its distance from the Sun. The formula worked for every observation that he had record of, and Kepler was delighted with this new law that he saw as strong evidence of the ultimate harmony and perfection of the universe.

As it has turned out, Kepler's laws of planetary motion hold true for celestial bodies that Kepler didn't know about and had never even conceived of. When Galileo later first spotted the four large moons of Jupiter through his telescope, observation showed that they, too, moved around the planet according to the same principles that Kepler had found for the planets revolving around the Sun. And, many years later, when multiple star systems were discovered, they, too, were found to follow the same laws.

Kepler's three laws also signaled an important change in science. Unlike the Greeks and many others after them, Kepler made no attempt to explain *why* the planets moved, only *how*. He made use of mathematics and observational data to talk about their movements, and, as science writer Bruce Gregory puts it, "Kepler went far beyond simply summarizing the description of planetary motions; he invented a way of talking about the motion of heavenly bodies that is still valuable today."

Kepler attempted no scientific explanation of what caused the movement of the planets, but he was greatly interested in William Gilbert's work on magnetism, published in 1601, and Kepler's work shows that he suspected the Sun operated some kind of physical control, that magnetic action kept the planets orbiting about it.

LEGACY OF A TRIAD

In the end, these three men, Copernicus, Tycho and Kepler began a true revolution in the way people thought about the world. They all did science for the sheer love of it (none of them earned his living at it; the day of the professional modern scientist was yet to come). And it is also important to remember that each of these scientists, building on the contributions of the one who came before, made important progress despite his own various foibles. This point is key to what science is all about and how it works.

Copernicus apparently clung to the Aristotelian idea of crystalline spheres and the idea that the stars hung on an outer sphere. He did not imagine, as we know today, that, beyond Earth's atmosphere, space is an infinite vacuum and that the closest star is 4.5 light years away. Nonetheless—as often happens in science—he was bothered by the way observed facts failed to fit with theory. As a result, he thought: Maybe we are looking at this whole thing from the wrong perspective. What if the Sun, not the Earth, is at the center? And then he followed through by making calculations to see if his theory worked. It didn't quite work. But it came a lot closer than anyone else's ideas ever had before, and he gave those who followed him some good ideas to build on.

Tycho believed adamantly in his compromise scheme that still put the Earth back in the center of things, and he was wrong. He collected his massive data bank of observations to prove he was right. And the data failed to prove his point. But, even though his theory was wrong, he made careful and honest observations, and those helped lead to new ideas about the universe that worked better than his. This is an important point in science: It doesn't matter if your hypothesis is wrong, as long as you are willing to test it, and allow others to test it, and repeat the tests. What is important is this process of postulating, testing, analyzing the results and reaching new conclusions based on the results. Tycho was a great collector of data, the most accurate and meticulous naked-eye astronomer of all time. In this he made an invaluable contribution to the sum of human knowledge.

Kepler thought that the orbits of the planets must be circular. He was a mystic, a Platonist, and his intuitive sense told him that this view of the Solar System must be correct. He, too, was wrong. He didn't abandon his vision of circular orbits for a long time—not until he had tried just about every version of the idea that he could think of. It's hard to let go of an assumption one is attached to. But finally he did, and he came up with another idea that turned out to work beautifully: the ellipse. So, building on the contributions of Copernicus and Tycho before him, Kepler was able to solve another piece of the puzzle of the universe and set the stage for those who came after him in the exciting years of the 17th century, the years of the scientific revolution in full bloom.

C H A P T E R   4

A "VAST AND MOST EXCELLENT SCIENCE": GALILEO AND THE BEGINNINGS OF METHOD

In questions of science the authority of a thousand is not worth the humble reasoning of a single individual.
—Galileo Galilei

Despite the breakthroughs made by Copernicus, Tycho and Kepler, the winds of tradition continued to blow against acceptance of new ideas about the universe. "Many years ago I became a convert to the opinions of Copernicus," the Italian scientist Galileo Galilei wrote to Johannes Kepler in 1597. Thoroughly convinced, he had found that, by using Copernicus's theory, he could explain many phenomena that Ptolemy's system had left "altogether inexplicable." But, Galileo confessed in that same letter, he had long held back from publishing his arguments out of fear that the world would laugh at him as it had at Copernicus. "I should indeed dare to bring forward my speculations," he confided to Kepler, "if there were many like you; but since there are not, I shrink from a subject of this description."

Anyone might easily imagine, from the sound of this letter to Kepler, that Galileo Galilei was a timid, shrinking man, unsure of his own observations and unwilling to put his thoughts and ideas on the line. In fact, the letter gives a better glimpse of the times he lived in than of the great scientist himself. In his prime, Galileo [gahl-ih-LAY-oh] (who was always called by his first name alone) was an irascible, stocky man with red hair, short of temper as well as stature, whose style of thought and work looms large in

Galileo Galilei
(Yerkes Observatory)

the history of science. He produced major insights about motion and mechanics and made breakthrough discoveries in astronomy. Most important of all, he revolutionized the way scientists approached their work. He also spent most of the last 20 years of his life at the center of a great controversy over the Copernican and Ptolemaic systems.

"Be of good cheer, Galileo," Kepler wrote back in reply, "and appear in public. If I am not mistaken there are only a few among the distinguished mathematicians of Europe who would dissociate themselves from us. So great is the power of truth." It was a rare optimistic burst from the usually gloomy younger man, and unfortunately Kepler underestimated the tenacity with which the conservative thinkers of the time would hold onto their traditional ideas.

Galileo was born in Pisa, Italy on February 15, 1564, the same year Shakespeare was born in England and three days before Michelangelo died. Like both of them, Galileo was a man of the Renaissance. He liked music and art, loved literature and poetry, played the lute and was accomplished enough with brush and watercolor to illustrate his own astronomical findings. He was also an excellent writer who wrote with a clear and dynamic style—a fact, ironically, that would end up counting against him. A more turgid and foggy stylist would have had fewer readers and would have presented much less threat to the established ways of thinking, no matter how strongly he might have established the proofs of his arguments. When Galileo wrote, his words bristled, and those whose ideas were being pricked could hardly fail to take notice.

The fiery Galileo was also very much a man of the world. Although he never married, he had three children—a son and two daughters—by his mistress, Marina Gamba. A man of strong personal convictions and passionate feelings, he loved his children, and when Marina finally married someone else, he took the children in and provided for them (not always an easy chore given his bachelor life-style). In his later years he made a point of living near the convent of his daughter, Virginia, who had become a nun.

As a boy Galileo moved with his family to Florence, the heart of Renaissance culture, where he lived until 1581, when he left for the University of Pisa to study medicine at the age of 17. His father, a none-too-wealthy mathematician, had encouraged Galileo to become a physician, a career he thought had better prospects than his own. (A physician had a potential income about 30 times higher than a mathematician's.)

While in Pisa one day, so the story goes, the young Galileo was sitting in the cathedral when he noticed the pendulum swing of the beautiful chandelier that hung from the ceiling. Already more attuned to observing and pondering the mysteries of nature than attending to the philosophical abstractions of religious ritual, he became engrossed with the motion of the pendulum's swing. Timing it against his pulse, he noticed that, for as long as he watched it, the chandelier completed the same number of swings in the same number of pulse beats. The arc of pendulum swings might become shorter as time passed, but the elapsed time from the beginning of one swing to the beginning of the next always remained the same. Later, at home, young Galileo pushed the point further. To verify his observations he set up a simple set of experiments. He tried pendulums tied with weights of different sizes. He made them swing in wide arcs, in medium arcs and in small arcs, always timing against his pulse (the best time measurement he had at that point). The number of swings in a given length of time never varied unless he changed the length of the string.

Galileo had found out something basic about movement and dynamics. But, even more important was his method: Instead of just reasoning his ideas through logically, in the manner of most of the Greeks and his contemporaries—the scientists or "natural philosophers" of his day—he measured time and distance and *introduced mathematics into physics*. Then he tested and proved his point by experiment.

WILLIAM GILBERT:
PIONEER OF EXPERIMENTAL SCIENCE

Although Galileo often gets the credit for being the first major thinker to regularly employ the new scientific methods of observation and experiment in his investigations, he was not without predecessors. One of the most important of these was the English physician and physicist William Gilbert (1544–1603).

No one knows for sure when people first discovered magnetic stones, but they had been a source of curiosity for many centuries. Legends say that the first such object was discovered by a shepherd near the Asian city of Magnesia, where many centuries later such stones came to be called Magnesian stones, or magnets, by the English. Similar stones were studied by the Greek philosopher Thales, but it was the Chinese who first discovered that if a magnetic sliver was allowed to turn freely it would point in a north-south position. The Chinese, though, were not much interested in great seafaring expeditions, and it was the English, some time in the 12th century, who eventually developed the magnetic compass that later became such a great aid in helping England to become a major world power.

Magnetism was still a very mysterious force in the 16th and 17th centuries. And, although Peter Peregrinus, a pupil of the English scientist Roger Bacon, had studied magnets in the 13th century, the first man to make such a study in a long series of carefully detailed experiments and observations was William Gilbert.

Also, *anyone could repeat Galileo's experiment and get the same results*—another principle that became key to the new "scientific method." Although others including Francis Bacon and William Gilbert had championed this method, Galileo was really the first to use consistently this repeatable and verifiable approach. He was at the vanguard of a major feature of 17th-century science: The idea that the laws of nature are mathematical, and that the approach of the scientists must therefore be mathematical.

In this, as science historians like to say, Galileo was closer to Archimedes than any other predecessor—Archimedes, who, in the third century B.C., much against the currents of his own time, had achieved insights into the way levers work and principles of floating objects by observing real objects and then abstracting what he saw into mathematical formulas.

In fact, Galileo loved mathematics so much that he finally succeeded in switching careers, in spite of his father's hopes to the contrary. But the

A brilliant physician who eventually reached the envious position of president of the College of Physicians, Gilbert is known today for his experiments with magnets and magnetism. His book *De magnete* (*About Magnets*), published in 1600, is still considered one of the first classics of experimental science and was greatly admired by Galileo, who wrote, "I think him worthy of the greatest praise for the many new and true observations which he has made, to the disgrace of so many vain and fabling authors, who write not from their own knowledge only, but repeat everything they hear from the foolish and vulgar, without attempting to satisfy themselves of the same by experiment."

Gilbert's many results from his experiments also led him to conclude that the Earth itself behaved like a giant magnet with its magnetic poles very near its geographic poles. He also postulated from his experience with various magnets that the Earth probably turned on its axis, although he demonstrated little interest in the Copernican theory that the Earth also revolved around the Sun. And, although his experiments led him to many new discoveries about magnets, including the similar attractive properties of amber and other materials when rubbed with fur, Gilbert still assumed that their "power" was due to some mysterious and perhaps "living" force that resided within them.

Gilbert's researches into magnetics and their properties were not surpassed until well into the 18th century when researchers began to investigate more closely the properties of magnetism and electricity.

strong-minded Galileo was not always the easiest person to get along with and had by this time succeeded in alienating many of his professors at the University of Pisa with his constant challenges to the ancient authorities. In those days, an excellent student was expected to be able to recite word-for-word from the works of the ancients and apply without question these accepted ideas. From the academics' point of view, "thinking for oneself" was a useless and disrespectful waste of time, since the ancients had already figured everything out. So, although Galileo had impressed Ostilio Ricci, a great mathematician of the time, and had a brief opportunity to study with him, he failed to obtain a scholarship he needed and, no longer able to afford to stay in Pisa, he withdrew from the university without a degree and returned home to Florence in 1586.

For anyone with less determination and brilliance, the story could have ended there, with dashed hopes and no career. But, continuing his studies of mathematics, that same year Galileo published a brief pamphlet about a mechanism he had invented, a hydrostatic balance that measured the pressure in a fluid. As a result, and through his father's connections, he attracted the attention of several influential noblemen, one of whom, the Marquis Guidoboldo del Monte, pulled a few strings and helped him secure his first academic position in 1589, a junior post in mathematics back at the University of Pisa. There, of course, no one had forgotten his previous reputation—only three years had passed since his notorious student days—and Galileo, outspoken and cocksure as ever, did little to enhance his popularity with his fellow faculty members. Meanwhile, his father died in 1591, leaving young Galileo with financial responsibility for his mother and six brothers and sisters. His three-year contract would soon be up, and he had good reason to believe it would not be renewed. But his friend, the Marquis del Monte, came through for him again and in 1592, Galileo's salary was tripled when he was offered the chair in mathematics at the famous University of Padua in the Republic of Venice.

In Padua Galileo, never lacking in self-esteem, also seems to have found his style. He taught in the Auditorium Maximum (the "large auditorium") to packed audiences of students and young representatives of noble houses from all over Europe, including Gustavus Adolphus, the crown prince of Sweden. He taught practical applications of mathematical principles, such as how to build bridges, plan harbors, fortify cities and buildings and construct artillery. But Galileo's big draw as a teacher was that, instead of dry, droning lectures on these subjects, he performed careful and often dramatic demonstrations for his classes. He showed students how things worked, instead of merely studying ancient manuscripts and comparing passages of texts to try to ferret out the truths of nature from the minds of other men. He demonstrated to his class how, if he whistled to an organ pipe, it would imitate his sound by answering with the same note: resonance. He showed how when pistols were fired on a mountain, one could count the seconds between the time they were fired and the time the report was heard—illustrating that sound travels at speeds that can be measured. He took animal bones to class to demonstrate that strong construction supports did not have to be solid—giving birth to hollow-pipe construction, which enabled builders to bring construction costs down dramatically. He told his students to seek truth in nature, and showed them how to use their own eyes, minds, mathematics and experiments, not merely ancient and revered manuscripts, to find that truth.

DISCOVERING LAWS OF MOTION

Galileo is probably most famous for three events: dropping two cannonballs of different size from the Leaning Tower of Pisa, inventing the telescope and being martyred for his beliefs about the Copernican system. All three of these, however, have been passed down in legend at least slightly skewed; yet all three stories also contain a large element of truth.

First, the story of the cannonballs. Aristotle thought that heavier objects "naturally" fell faster than lighter objects. And that idea seemed perfectly obvious to most thinkers of his time and for centuries afterward. After all, anyone could observe that a feather, for example, falls more slowly than a rock. According to the cannonball story, Galileo took a cannonball and a musketball—the same shape as a cannonball but smaller and lighter—to the top of the Leaning Tower of Pisa, let them both drop and timed their descent to the ground. When they both hit the ground at the same time he had proved, the story goes, that two objects of different weight do not necessarily fall at different rates, after all. A colorful story, but probably not true. It first appeared in a biography written by one of his students, Vincenzio Viciani, who tended to exaggerate, and Galileo never wrote about this particular experiment himself.

He did, however, establish that objects fall at almost exactly the same rate, regardless of their comparative weights. What makes the difference between a falling rock's rate of fall and a feather's is not their weight but air resistance.

And Galileo did write about a series of experiments he made with sloping surfaces (inclined planes, or ramps) and rolling balls. He decided to use these

According to legend, Galileo experimented by dropping unevenly matched weights— a cannonball and a musketball—from the Leaning Tower of Pisa at the same time.

ramps because he had no good way of measuring the rapid speed and acceleration of objects such as cannonballs in free fall. To measure time he used a water clock, a system that measured time with dripping water, much as an hourglass does with sand. The ramps, fitted out with polished grooves to keep the balls moving in a straight line, slowed the movement down enough so that he could time the balls' descents accurately, even with his water clock. And, even though the balls were moving along a sloping surface, he recognized that their movement was essentially the same as free fall.

As they rolled down the ramp, the balls seemed to accelerate, or speed up, in a predictable way, adding the same amount of additional speed with every second of travel. For example, if the ball traveled 1 meter in one second, it traveled 3 in the next second and 5 in the next. So after 2 seconds of travel, the ball would have traveled a total of 4 meters, and a total of 9 meters after 3 seconds. No matter how much he experimented, the results were always the same. The increase in velocity was always the same; the acceleration remained constant. Galileo summed this up in one of his first laws of motion: "The spaces passed over in natural motion are in proportion to the squares of the times." Today we usually refer to Galileo's discovery as the law of uniform acceleration. It states simply that, excluding the effects of air resistance, the rate of acceleration is always the same.

Throughout his lifetime, Galileo explored questions surrounding motion and mechanics. Already, as far back as 1590, Galileo had written a work he called *De motu gravium* ("On the motion of heavy bodies"). In it he updated Aristotle's basic thoughts about motion, using some ideas put forth 300 years earlier by Jean Buridan (c. 1295–1358). For centuries thinkers had struggled to understand why an arrow flew, a question that Aristotle had answered poorly with his theory of projectile motion (the movement of something thrown or shot, such as a ball, an arrow or a bullet). Aristotle believed that everything returned to its natural state. But an arrow or a thrown stone keeps traveling horizontally, once released. Because Aristotle insisted that movement required direct contact with a propelling force, he had come to the conclusion that the air, pushed aside by the moving object, rushed in behind it, providing the impetus (or driving force) that kept it traveling along. Buridan, who studied under William of Ockham, contested this Aristotelian scenario. He thought that the thrust of the original driving force, all by itself, was enough to keep an object moving forever, without help from the movement of air. He also thought that what held true on Earth also held true in the heavens. And he translated his ideas about motion to the heavens, where he thought the spheres, once set in motion by God, needed no further help from angels to keep them moving, as many other medieval scholars believed.

Picking up, in part, from where Buridan left off, Galileo came up with a new theory of impetus: Without resistance a violent motion will persist with constant velocity (speed and direction combined). Or, put more simply, in a vacuum (where there is no resistance created by atmosphere), once an object is set moving, it will continue at the same speed and in the same direction until something intervenes to change its speed or direction.

By the time he was finished, Galileo ended up throwing out many of Aristotle's ideas. He never really let go, though, of Aristotle's idea that objects moved in response to their own "desires" or innate tendencies—that a rock, for example, falls to the ground because it "wants" to return to its natural state. As rebellious and independent as he was, Galileo didn't see that the way objects moved resulted purely from their inertial mass and the application of force. That would come later with the work of Isaac Newton.

As Galileo continued working through his ideas about the nature of motion, he also set forth the idea that objects on the Earth's surface are not affected by the planet's movement (in defense of Copernican heliocentrism). But even Galileo had his blind spots, claiming that the movement of the tides showed that Copernicus was right, that the Earth was moving and not stationary—a contradiction within his own argument.

THE TELESCOPE: SEEING IS BELIEVING

As for Galileo and the invention of the telescope, he was not, in fact, the inventor. In about 1609 he heard about a device made by a spectacle-maker in Flanders, a pipe fitted with lenses through which one could look and see details on ships still far out at sea—even sailors climbing the rigging. Galileo deduced from the rumors how it must have been designed and constructed one of his own. But if he was not the first to make a telescope, he was unquestionably the first to think of using it systematically to study the skies, instead of merely using it to spot ships at sea or to observe troop movements in battle. He turned his newly magnified sight toward the Moon, the stars (including the Milky Way) and the planets. And what he saw stirred great excitement in 17th-century Europe.

The Moon, he discovered, was not a smooth and perfect sphere as most astronomers and philosophers since Aristotle had supposed. "I feel sure," he wrote, based on his observations, "that the surface of the moon is not perfectly smooth, free from inequalities, and exactly spherical, as a large school of philosophers considers . . . The grandeur . . . of such prominences and depressions in the moon seems to surpass both in magnitude and extent the ruggedness of the earth's surface." In fact, he saw, the Moon had great mountains and dark areas he called *maria* or "seas" (although we now know there is not one drop of water on the Moon).

Then one night to his amazement, as he gazed at the planet Jupiter, close to the planet he spied three—then a few weeks later, four—unknown worlds, which he called new "stars." No one had ever seen them before. Known today as Jupiter's "Galilean" moons, named in his honor, these were the four enormous moons that orbit in the giant planet's system: Io, Europa, Ganymede and Callisto. But they are too small to be seen with the naked eye; this was the first time anyone had used enough magnification to see them.

The discovery of Jupiter's moons held special implications for Copernicus's view of the Solar System. Many detractors had attacked the Copernican system with the argument that, if Earth was not at the center of the universe, then why did Earth alone have a moon circling about it in orbit? Now Galileo had found another planet with not one but four circling moons. Maybe Copernicus's view of things was not so foolish, after all.

Many other discoveries followed. He turned his telescope toward Venus, and saw that, like the Moon, this planet also had phases—from crescent to disc to crescent. He concluded that, like the Moon, Venus must not shine with its own light, but with light reflected from the Sun. The new observations of Venus also seemed to fit with Copernicus's revolutionary ideas, as Kepler had modified them. Galileo's telescope it seemed was making Copernicus's "outlandish ideas" seem more likely every day.

In 1610 Galileo published his observations in a book he called *Sidereus nuncius* (*The Messenger of the Stars*). As a result he enjoyed considerable fame, success—and notoriety. He became "philosopher and chief mathematician" to the grand duke of Tuscany, Cosimo II de' Medici. He was elected to an elite group of scientists called the *Accademia dei Lincei* (Academy of the Lynx-eyed), named after the animal traditionally thought to be the most keen-sighted of all. And, of course, Galileo attracted not a little jealousy from his peers.

ARGUMENT AND CAPITULATION: THE TRIAL

Given the temper of the times, it was inevitable that Galileo's discoveries and writings would soon come under criticism as offensive to religion. Worse yet, it seemed that his popular writing style was winning converts not only to the Copernican system but to an entirely new and troubling way of thinking about nature. In 1616, the Holy Office of the Church at Rome condemned the idea that the Sun was at the center of the cosmos and, exerting its tremendous power, specifically forbade Galileo to teach Copernican theory or defend it in writing.

Strangely enough a few years later, when the church sought to rewrite the works of Copernicus to fit better with current theology, Galileo, perhaps

GIORDANO BRUNO: MARTYR FOR SCIENCE?

Many accounts of science history invoke the fate of a Dominican friar named Giordano Bruno as a prime example of the enormous struggles suffered by early scientists in the 16th and 17th centuries at the hands of religious authorities. But, technically speaking, Bruno was not a bona fide participant in this new and exciting way of looking at the world.

A strange, dark and brooding man, Bruno was born the son of a poor soldier near Naples, Italy in 1548. After attending the University of Naples, he entered a Dominican monastery in 1563. A radical thinker as well as a devoted mystic, Bruno was a fiery public speaker, and his outspoken pronouncements on a variety of subjects the church saw as heretical often put him in danger from the authorities. Constantly on the run, and constantly developing more and more extremely mystical and fanatic ideas, he fled from Rome to Geneva, sought solace in Paris and wandered all over Europe. Along his travels he also lectured in England and Germany before being arrested finally in Venice in 1592.

Bruno's philosophy was a hodgepodge of ideas, which included believing that space is infinite and that there might be people on other worlds in the universe. It is this belief that usually finds him included in popular books on science history. There is little evidence, however, that Bruno arrived at these conclusions through a logical or scientific process. Instead, they were just examples of the many ideas, often contradictory, from which he wove his somewhat incoherent brand of personal mysticism.

Giordano Bruno was burned at the stake in Rome in 1600 after a seven-year trial. He refused up to the last to recant, even, according to some accounts, turning down a cross that was offered him as the stakes were lit. While some popular books claim that Bruno's execution was due to his belief in the infinity of space and the inhabitability of other planets, these were insignificant items on his long list of what the church considered dangerous heresies. He was, unquestionably, a martyr in the cause of free speech and thought. But as a hero in the cause of early science, he falls short.

---

thinking that his superior arguments would set things right, and perhaps believing that the church was adopting a more liberal position, volunteered to do the job.

In 1632 he published *Dialogue on the Two Chief Systems of the World.* His presentation took the form of a debate among three characters, one of them

Frontispiece of Galileo's Dialogue on the Two Chief Systems of the World, *showing a heated, though imaginary, discussion among Aristotle (left), Ptolemy and Copernicus (right)— who of course could not have met* (Smithsonian Institution Libraries)

a speaker defending Copernicus and another speaking for Aristotle. Galileo claimed that he meant to show a fair and even battle. But the speaker for Aristotle was called Simplicio—which offers a clear clue to what Galileo really thought. The arguments for Copernicus's ideas, meanwhile, were more closely reasoned and better spoken. The authorities of the church were outraged. With Protestantism nipping at its heels, the Catholic church couldn't afford to look as if it were abandoning tradition. And more importantly, the church authorities could not afford to show weakness.

At the age of 70, Galileo was summoned to Rome. He was charged with heresy for his belief that "the Sun is in the center of the world and immovable, and the Earth is not the center." The church had seen through his attempts to sidestep the 1616 directive. As for the issue of who was right about the way the world really works, most of Galileo's opponents refused even to look through Galileo's telescope or listen to his reasoning. His proof through observation was still a new approach, and they believed they already knew the truth. If Galileo's telescope showed something else then, they argued, there must be a flaw in the telescope and why should they waste their time? Galileo had been courageous and persistent in his beliefs but he had also pushed his luck, and, of course, he had never been known for his tact.

In Rome he was found guilty of heresy and sentenced to prison. Finally, at the church of Santa Maria Sopra Minerva, fearing torture, he capitulated in his famous public apology: "I do not hold and have not held this opinion of Copernicus since the command was intimated to me that I must abandon it."

According to legend, as the frail and elderly scientist walked away from that moment, he muttered obstinately under his breath, "Nevertheless the Earth does move!" But, while Galileo may have been stubborn, he knew who held the cards. The powerful church had won the battle. And Galileo, who may have been occasionally foolhardy, was no fool. What he may have been thinking at that moment we will never know, but it is unlikely, given the situation, that he really said anything of the sort. It is a tribute to the power of his personality and his highly individualistic mark on history that the legend lives on without any evidence to substantiate it.

Although he was never actually imprisoned, Galileo's great book was banned and he spent the rest of his life under house arrest at Arcetri, where he was visited by, among others, the young poet John Milton and influenced the development of the philosopher Thomas Hobbes. Despite the displeasure of the church, he had carved a niche for himself in world history, and he knew it. As he put it, he had "opened up to this vast and most excellent science, of which my work is merely the beginning, ways and means by which other minds more acute than mine will explore its remotest corners."

"Pure logical thinking," Albert Einstein once wrote, "cannot yield us any knowledge of the empirical world; all knowledge of reality starts from experience and ends in it. . . . Because Galileo saw this, and particularly because he drummed it into the scientific world, he is the father of modern physics—indeed, of modern science altogether."

Galileo Galilei died on January 8, 1642, in the same year that another great scientist, Isaac Newton, was born in England.

NEWTON, THE LAWS OF MOTION AND THE "NEWTONIAN REVOLUTION"

If I have seen further it is by standing on the shoulders of giants.
—Isaac Newton

The death of Galileo in 1642 marked the end of an age. In Italy Galileo had laid groundwork for a powerful new "scientific method." But even during Galileo's own time, and certainly by the time of his death, the great Renaissance in Italy had begun to draw to a close. And by 1642, Italy no longer offered the best training ground for scientists.

Elsewhere in Europe and England, new political structures had emerged to replace the old feudal societies, nation-states with more or less unified policies. In Italy, however, the old city-states still retained their animosities and could not seem to draw together to form a similar strength. Meanwhile, toward the end of the 15th century, a way had been found to travel by ship around Africa's Cape of Good Hope, establishing trade routes to the East that replaced the overland routes through the Middle East on which Italy had so long held a monopoly. By 1661, the English acquired Bombay, and trade with India vastly increased as a result. And, ironically, the New World across the Atlantic, discovered to Europeans by Italian Christopher Columbus in 1492, also began, by the mid-17th century, to fatten the coffers of England and its North European neighbors. Columbus, of course, had not sailed under an Italian flag—there was no unified Italian state and no state with sufficient finances and interest to send him. Italy and Greece were no longer at the center of the Western world. And the spirit of expansion that became prevalent to the North—in England, France, the Netherlands—now provided better soil for new advances in science to grow in.

In addition, the heavily repressive attitudes of the Roman Catholic Counter-Reformation made far less impact in the North. In 1534 England had established the independent Church of England, with the king of England, not the pope, at its head. By 1642, a series of civil wars, also known as the Puritan Revolution, pushed even further for the cause of freedom of thought. Even though England returned to monarchy in 1660, the conflict of ideas on the political and religious fronts introduced an intellectual turbulence that fostered independent thought and new ideas.

THE GREAT SYNTHESIZER

This was the world into which Isaac Newton was born, on December 25, 1642. The scene was a farm in the village of Woolsthorpe in Lincolnshire, a largely agricultural county in eastern England. Born prematurely, he was

Isaac Newton
(Yerkes Observatory)

so tiny that his mother liked to say he would have fit in a quart mug. He spent a lonely childhood; his father died before he was born and his mother, who remarried when Newton was three, gave him over to his grandmother for care during most of his early years. Young Isaac amused himself making gadgets, such as kites carrying lit candles that flared through the sky, water clocks and sundials. He boarded for awhile with a pharmacist and there became fascinated with alchemy, which was still the chemistry of the time. He showed curiosity but no great intellectual promise in school—at least not until he got into a brawl with the school bully, who also happened to be at the top of his class. Always contentious and concerned with issues of pride, Newton suddenly began to pour himself into his studies to compete.

Newton's mother, whose second husband had also died by this time, had always assumed that her son would take over running the farm. But when he left school to turn his hand to farming, it became clear that he had no real aptitude for it, taking every opportunity to hole up with his books instead. And so, thanks to the insight of an uncle who was a member of Trinity College at Cambridge, he was sent to Cambridge University, which he attended from 1660 until he graduated in 1665. Still, however, even at the age of 23, Isaac Newton had shown no special brilliance. No clue could yet be detected that he would become the great unifier of the scientific revolution, drawing from the ideas of Copernicus, Kepler, Galileo and others. No sign yet showed of the great advances he would make in theoretical physics and the understanding of bodies in motion. And he betrayed no indication of the great contributions he would make to the fields of optics and mathematics.

But in 1665 bubonic infection—the Great Plague—hit London, virtually shutting that city down. Cambridge soon followed and Newton left the university for the comparative safety of the farm in Lincolnshire, where, in a forced 18-month vacation, he began putting together some ideas. The results marked the beginning of a long and fruitful career in science—one of the few positive legacies of the deadly plagues that swept Europe in his time. During this period he laid the foundations for the calculus, a mathematical method of calculation that would revolutionize scientists' ability to handle complicated equations. And it was also during this time that he noticed an apple falling to the ground (although it doubtless did not hit him on the head as legend claims). The event set him to wondering if the force that pulled the apple toward the Earth might be the same as the one that kept the Moon in orbit. This notion represented a big break with the traditions of Aristotle, who had insisted that the Earth and the heavens operated on two entirely different sets of laws. Newton began to see that apples follow the same natural laws as the Moon and that there is only one, universal set of laws, not two.

During his forced stay in the country, Newton also did a fascinating series of experiments with light. At that time everyone assumed that white light was the absence of color. To test this he set a prism in front of a crack in a heavy curtain in a darkened room so that sunlight would stream through it onto a screen. The light separated out into all the colors of the rainbow, red, orange, yellow, green, blue and violet. Where did these colors come from? Were they created in the prism? Newton suspected that they were the components of the light itself, so he passed the refracted light, the rainbow "spectrum," through a second prism turned in the opposite direction. The colors recombined, and a spot of clear, white light appeared on the screen.

Newton returned to Cambridge in 1667 and became professor of mathematics there in 1669. Already, by the age of 25 when he returned to Cambridge, Isaac Newton had marked out the areas of his life's work. But he was not working in isolation. He lived in a time of great scientific interest, filled with challenges, exchanges and debates. In 1662 a band of science enthusiasts in England had founded a prestigious group called the Royal Society to further the cause of science. Each week its members presented experiments and new findings. By 1675 they succeeded in persuading the king to build a Royal Observatory; England's need for accurate navigation maps justified building facilities to draw more accurate maps of the skies. And John Flamsteed (1646–1719), England's first astronomer royal, set about making meticulous tables of star positions and star maps. In 1672 Newton was elected to membership in the Royal Society, where he presented his experiments on light and optics.

Robert Hooke (1635–1703), curator of the society, had done some similar experiments—though not as thorough and conclusive as Newton's—and immediately took offense. In 1665 he had published his wave theory of light in his work *Micrographia*, comparing the dissemination of light to waves in water. He also had proposed a color theory, working with colors of membranes and observing light through thin plates of mica. But his observations took in only two colors, red and blue, and his explanations fell short. Nevertheless, he felt that Newton had stepped on his territory, and a life-long animosity began.

Newton was never on very cordial terms with any of his contemporaries; the loner child remained a loner all his life, never marrying, always slightly paranoid and unquestionably contentious. So he did not, in many cases, work closely with other scientists or collaborate. He did, however, as he was the first to admit, draw from others, pulling together, clarifying and synthesizing methods and theories that seemed valid but contradictory.

The scientific methods of Newton's countryman Francis Bacon (1561–1626), born nearly 100 years before him, and French philosopher René Descartes (1596–1650) make a good example. In 1620, Bacon proposed what is now called the inductive, or *a posteriori*, approach to reasoning. Like

Galileo, he believed that scientific ideas must be based on first-hand observation and experiment. And conclusions about universal truths should be drawn based on observed particulars. He maintained that deductive, or *a priori*, reasoning, the kind of "armchair" philosophy the Greeks had indulged in so much, had led thinkers astray for too long. Bacon's ideas gained strength, since they fit well with his country's religious position, which emphasized personal religious experience over dogma, and with the Industrial Revolution in the following century, which would serve to strengthen England's growing economic power.

In France, meanwhile, Descartes, 35 years younger than Bacon, in many ways provided a counterpoint with his *Discours sur la méthode* (*Discourse on Method*), published in 1637. He established the deductive method of reasoning, in which *a priori* reasoning plays a key part, working from the general to the particular.

For Descartes, the key question was how does anyone know anything? How, for example, do I know that I exist? In his *Discourse* he concluded, finally, "Cogito ergo sum" ("I think, therefore I am"). He set forth the idea of a mechanistic universe, created by God, but running according to laws established from the beginning. (He stopped short of the idea that, after setting the universe in motion, God no longer intervenes; that was an idea that would come later, in the Age of the Enlightenment.) The universe, he maintained, was made up of two types of matter—created, or "extensive," matter and the Soul-substance of thinking beings (humans)—and this duality became an important part of Cartesian philosophy (named after Descartes). Descartes held tremendous sway in 17th-century Europe, despite what seemed in some ways like a return to the old Greek ways.

But René Descartes was also the first to attempt a comprehensive scheme of the universe expressed mathematically. Not the least of his contributions was the analytical geometry he invented, which made possible much more complex calculations than had ever been possible before. Until the introduction of calculus to the arsenal of mathematics, this was the greatest breakthrough in the quantitative tools of science since the Greek classical age.

From these two legacies Isaac Newton, in turn, would take the experimentalism and inductive approach of Bacon, Galileo and Gilbert, combine it with the quantitative approach of Descartes and forge a new, even stronger method, applying mathematical tools to arrive at and frame experimental results.

Descartes also made an attempt to explain the problem introduced by Kepler's work, the great mystery of the age: why the planets move in elliptical orbits. In this, oddly enough, his approach was more descriptive than mathematical. Descartes maintained, like the Aristotelians, that no such thing as a vacuum existed, that a great vortex or whirlpool of fluid or ether carried the planets around the Sun. And he went further: Though God

FONTENELLE: THE FIRST PROFESSIONAL POPULAR SCIENCE WRITER

Although others had written books and articles on science aimed at the educated reader, Bernard le Bovier de Fontenelle (1657–1757) was the first nonscientist to devote his entire career to the writing of books and articles explaining science to the ordinary man and woman. Born in Rouen, France, the son of a lawyer, Fontenelle [fohnt-NEL] qualified for the law but abandoned it to become a writer. After only modest success in writing poetry and drama he became interested in science. His first book in the field of popular science writing was an introduction to new discoveries in astronomy, entitled *Entretiens sur la pluralité des mondes* (*Conversations on the Plurality of Worlds*), published in 1686. An immediate success, it was continually updated and republished for many years. As a strong supporter of the philosophical and scientific views of Descartes, Fontenelle never fully accepted the views of Newton. He was, however, an accomplished and easygoing stylist, and his writing helped to inform many readers about the scientific activities and theories of his time. Not limited to the "big cosmological picture," he wrote on many fields and scientists, illuminating just about all areas he touched. After becoming a member of the Académie des Sciences—a high honor—in 1696, he began a 42-year association as Perpetual Secretary to the Académie. It was in this position that he did his greatest and most famous work, the *Histoires,* summarizing the work of his scientific contemporaries in all fields, and a long series of *Eloges* ("Eulogies") of famous scientists presented after their deaths. Gifted in temperament as well as talent, Fontenelle was both a curious and a happy man, loving his work and doing it exceedingly well. His own death came quietly and benevolently after a life well spent, one month short of his 100th birthday.

had set the basic laws of nature in motion, new stars, solar systems and planets could form from the moving vortices, the ever-moving motions of the physical universe. Descartes's mechanistic view of the universe established a strong hold on European thought in his day and set the stage for the Age of Enlightenment that followed in the 18th century. But he had spun out his ideas about ether and vortices from his "armchair"; they were purely descriptive theories without quantitative proof.

The problem of the elliptical orbits attracted the best minds of the century, among them Christiaan Huygens (1629–1695) of the Netherlands, whom some consider the greatest scientist, after Newton, of the latter half of the century. He was the first to come up with a quantitative estimate of

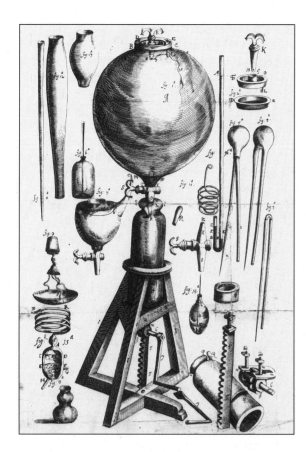

Air pump built by Robert Boyle and Robert Hooke for creating a vacuum
(Bancroft Library, University of California, Berkeley)

the amount of force required to move an object in a circle. Three members of the Royal Society—Robert Hooke, Christopher Wren (1632–1723) and Edmond Halley (1656–1742)—considered the case of a planet orbiting the Sun in the light of Huygens's results. They came up with a formula that accounted mathematically for a circular orbit around the Sun: If the force of attraction the Sun held on a planet was reduced in inverse proportion to the square of the distance, the planet would orbit in a circle. In other words, if Mars were twice as far from the Sun as Mercury, the attractive force exerted by the Sun on Mars would be one-fourth what it exerted on Mercury. If the more distant planet were four times as far from the Sun, the force would be one-sixteenth. But still no one had solved the mystery of the ellipse.

Halley, who was president of the Royal Society, had met Newton at Cambridge in 1684. Now he posed the question of the elliptical orbits to Newton. During his 18-month forced vacation on the family farm in 1665–66, Newton had already come to the same mathematical formula, the "inverse square" law, set forth by Hooke, Wren and Halley. In thinking about the apple and the Moon, both attracted by the Earth's force, he figured that the force would fall off according to the square of the distance from the center of the Earth. But when, to prove it, he had tried to figure how much farther the Moon was than the apple from the Earth's center, he ran into a flaw in the calculation and was stumped. So he had never published this work. But by now he had a revised figure for the radius of the Earth to work from, as well as more maturity and greater mathematical expertise. The result was Isaac Newton's greatest work, *Philosophiae naturalis principia mathematica*, or "The Mathematical Principles of Natural Philosophy" (known as the *Principia*), which he wrote in 18 months. The work, however, became the focus of another quarrel between Hooke and Newton, with Hooke pointing out that he had set forth the law of inverse square in a letter to Newton long before. The Royal Society backed off from its commitment to publish the work. But Halley stepped in, provided the money for publication, smoothed the quarrel temporarily between Hooke and Newton and even checked galleys. Only 2,500 copies were printed of that first edition, in three volumes, published in 1687.

THREE LAWS OF MOTION

Following in the footsteps of Copernicus, Kepler and Galileo, in the *Principia* Newton described a world view expressed in mathematical terms. In the first book he examined the laws governing motion, summarizing much of Galileo's work on this fundamental concept.

Galileo had realized that forces change the motion of objects, and that, if left alone, an object in motion would travel in a straight line forever. So to start with, in what became known as Newton's first law of motion, also known as the law of inertia, Newton summarized what Galileo had already said: An object at rest tends to stay at rest. An object in motion tends to continue in motion at constant speed in a straight line.

In his second law Newton states that the more force is placed on an object, the more it accelerates. But the more massive it is, the more it resists acceleration. This is why it's easier to throw a light rock than a heavy rock.

Finally, in this trio of insights, Newton stated his third law, that for every action there is an equal and opposite reaction. Or, when one object exerts a force on a second object, the second object exerts an equal but opposite force on the first. A rocket launch is a good example of Newton's third law at work. The rocket exerts a downward push on the exhaust gases, which push back, by Newton's third law. If the upward push of the exhaust gases exceeds the weight of the vehicle, the rocket rises off the launch pad into the air.

Newton was the first to differentiate between the mass and the weight of an object, two terms that many people still use interchangeably in everyday language, but that carry important differences in meaning in physics. The mass of a body is its resistance to acceleration. Or, another way to put it is that a body's mass is its quantity of inertia. The weight of a body is the amount of gravitational force between it and another body (for example, the Earth). A good example of how these two ideas are different is that in space, an astronaut's weight (the amount of gravitational force between the astronaut's body and the Earth) may be negligible. But the astronaut's mass (resistance to acceleration) remains the same as when he or she is standing on Earth. Newton's attention to the precision of language, along with his use of the universal language of mathematics, was an important contribution to the growth of science, which by this time had become complicated enough to require finer distinctions than ever before.

Newton used the three laws he set forth in Book One of the *Principia* as a basis for calculating the gravitational force between the Earth and the Moon. He came to the conclusion that it is directly proportional to the product of the masses of the two bodies and inversely proportional to the square of the distance between their centers. But what is more, he held that this law of attraction was the same throughout the universe. And he was able to show how this formula explained all of Kepler's laws.

In Book Two of the *Principia* Newton took on Descartes's vision of a universe filled with fluid, the motions of planets and stars governed by swirling vortices. This explanation of the universe seemed to answer many questions and had many supporters, especially in France and elsewhere on the European continent. But Newton found that when he applied quantitative methods to the theory, it wouldn't hold up. He explored mathematically the question of how fluids move and proved that the motions of a whirlpool could not "save the phenomena." Actual quantitative observations of the planets in motion did not match the way they would move if caught in a vortex of fluid. So Descartes's system did not work, after all.

The third and final book of Newton's *Principia* built on the first two in a very interesting way. If the laws and conclusions he had set forth were correct, Newton contended, then he should be able not only to explain observations that scientists had already made, but also to make predictions about phenomena that no one had yet observed. And he made some surprising projections.

For example, Newton had shown that the gravitational forces of the Earth's various parts combined to form a sphere. But, since the Earth is spinning around its axis, this additional force should disturb the perfect roundness of the sphere and create a bulge at the equator. Knowing the Earth's size, mass and rate of spin, he predicted the size of the bulge. During his lifetime efforts were made to verify this prediction and, because of errors

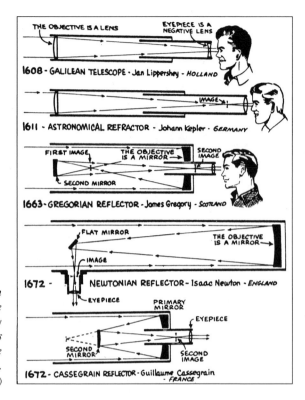

Developments in telescope design in the 17th century revolutionized ideas about the universe and its size.
(Edmund Scientific)

in calculation by mapmakers, he appeared to be wrong. But in fact, he was right about the bulge and his projection was accurate within one percent.

In a second famous prediction, he maintained that comets were not as mysterious as they seemed—that they also followed elliptical paths around the Sun, but that the paths were far more flattened and elongated than those pursued by the planets, taking them, possibly, even far beyond the edges of the Solar System.

This contention intrigued Edmond Halley, who in 1682 had observed the comet that bears his name and recognized a pattern in the appearances of comets about 75 to 76 years apart, which he guessed to be caused by the same comet reappearing at regular intervals. Based on this premise and Newton's calculations, he predicted that Halley's Comet would return in 76 years, in 1758. Of course, he was not alive—and neither was Newton—to see it, but Halley's Comet did return, as it has done regularly ever since, with its most recent appearance in 1986.

Many people think the *Principia* is the greatest book of science ever written. It tackled huge issues governing the overall scheme of the universe, using the new quantitative tools of the scientific revolution, culminating much of the great progress made in physics in the preceding two centuries.

Finally and forever it moved our ideas of the universe beyond the noble but limited efforts of the ancient Greeks, to a far more sophisticated and useful view. And, while Newton was not right about everything—He thought, for example, that "absolute motion" could exist, which Einstein later disproved with his theory of relativity—Newton's reasoning was sound and brilliantly incisive. In one fell swoop he had taken humankind's understanding of the universe a giant leap forward.

THE NATURE OF LIGHT

Newton's early experiments with light and optics caused him to consider the nature of light, which was another puzzling question of his time. While Huygens and Hooke both held that light, like sound, traveled in waves, Newton saw some problems with that idea (disagreeing, once again, with Hooke). While sounds can be heard around corners, one cannot see around a corner without the help of a mirror, and light can not usually be seen around a corner unless it is reflected, or bounced from a surface. So Newton went with Democritus in thinking that light was emitted by its source in a stream of particles, or "corpuscles," as he called them. This theory didn't explain all the evidence, but Newton was able to overcome most objections in his time, and his theory enabled scientists of the 18th century to make progress they might not have made using the "undulatory" or wave theory. Scientists experimenting in the 19th century, though, found that a wave theory of light explained their results better and they pegged Newton as wrong on this point. But current theories hold that light sometimes acts like particles, sometimes like waves—which explains why success in defining its nature was elusive for so long.

Perhaps wisely waiting until after the death of his rival Hooke, Newton published *Opticks*, a summary of his work on light, in 1704, in English this time instead of Latin as the *Principia* had been.

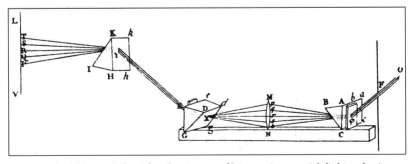

Drawing from Newton's Opticks, *showing one of his experiments with light and prisms*
(Isaac Newton: *Opticks: or, a Treatise of the Reflexions, Refractions, Inflexions and Colours of Light*, 1704)

SIR ISAAC NEWTON, HERO OF AN AGE

Halley once asked Newton how he managed to make so many discoveries. The key, Newton replied, was that he never relied on inspiration or serendipity to give him insights. He used intense focus and concentration and kept thinking relentlessly about problems that stumped him, never letting up—no doubt turning them over in his mind and exploring every angle during every available moment—until finally he worked out the answers.

His reputation for problem solving was so great that his work was recognizable even when he didn't sign his name. A Swiss scientist once proposed a set of problems as a contest, which Newton solved in a day and sent in anonymously. It could be none other than Newton, the delighted challenger insisted: "I recognized the claw of the lion." Wilhelm Leibniz once devised a complicated problem for the express purpose of stumping Newton. But Newton had the stickler solved in a single afternoon.

Newton quarreled often and pettily, it is true—with Hooke, with Huygens, with Leibniz over who invented the calculus first (they both came to it independently at about the same time), and with John Flamsteed over access to the astronomer royal's copious astronomical observations. He shabbily encouraged his friends to join the fray, providing them with ammunition for debate, stoking the fires of their anger, but rarely standing up in contention himself. Admirers often rankle to see Newton's greatness marred by these graceless squabbles and ugly controversies, as if a person who had soared so high should somehow be superhuman in every way. But maybe Newton's ego, which caused so many unflattering quarrels, also drove him to the intense concentration that produced the enormous results from which we still profit today. In any case, Isaac Newton was human, not a god. And that fact alone should challenge the rest of us to reach for heights like his.

In 1689 Newton became a member of Parliament, and in 1696 he became warden of the mint, which he revolutionized. Three years later, having by this time left his post at Cambridge, he became master of the mint. By 1703, Newton was elected president of the Royal Society, a position he retained until his death. And in 1705 he was knighted by Queen Anne.

Sir Isaac Newton died in London on March 20, 1727 and received a hero's burial in Westminster Abbey. Voltaire, an influential French philosopher, who was visiting in England at the time, expressed great wonderment at the English, who had treated a mathematician with the respect most countries would give only to a king. He carried his enthusiasm for Newton back to France, where he helped to disseminate his work, with the help of Emilie du Châtelet, who translated the *Principia* into French.

Emilie du Châtelet, who translated Newton's work into French and was largely responsible for the spread of his influence in Europe (The Bettmann Archive)

As Albert Einstein, the great 20th-century scientist who resolved many of the questions that Newton's physics left unanswered, wrote in a foreword to an edition of Newton's *Opticks:*

Nature was to him an open book, whose letters he could read without effort. The conceptions which he used to reduce the material of experience to order seemed to flow spontaneously from experience itself, from the beautiful experiments which he ranged in order like playthings and describes with an affectionate wealth of detail. In one person he combined the experimenter, the theorist, the mechanic and, not least, the artist in exposition. He stands before us strong, certain, and alone: his joy in creation and his minute precision are evident in every word and every figure.

Isaac Newton was, without question, one of the greatest scientists of all time, the crowning apex of the scientific revolution.

PART THREE

THE LIFE SCIENCES

THE ANATOMISTS: FROM VESALIUS TO FABRICIUS

*T*he same year that Nicolaus Copernicus published his famous book *De revolutionibus orbium coelestium*, Andreas Vesalius published his masterwork *De humani corporis fabrica* ("Concerning the Structure of the Human Body"). Together, these two books, one presenting a revolutionary new look at the structure of the heavens, the other the first major study of the anatomy of the human body since the days of the Roman Empire, made the year 1543 a watershed in the scientific revolution.

In *De revolutionibus*, Copernicus challenged the traditional view of the Earth-centered universe and the theories of Ptolemy that had been held sacred for more than a thousand years. Andreas Vesalius, meanwhile, threw down the gauntlet in the *Fabrica* to challenge the intellectual hold of the ancients upon the medical minds of the 16th century.

Medicine, like astronomy, was dominated in those days by the ideas and writing of one individual, whose words, preserved through the centuries, had become unquestioned and undisputed "laws." In astronomy that man was Ptolemy. In medicine that man was Galen, a Greek physician born in Asia Minor in about A.D. 130.

GALEN'S MIXED LEGACY

Bright, articulate and self-assured, Galen [GAY-len] had received the finest education money could buy. By the age of 18 he had already finished two years in the study of medicine and was well educated in the philosophies of Plato and Aristotle as well as the ideas of the Stoics and Epicureans. After spending the next few years continuing his medical studies in Greece, Phoenicia, Palestine, Crete, Cyprus and Alexandria, he finished his studies in A.D. 158 and returned to set up practice in his home town of Pergamum (modern Bergama, Turkey). It was there, over the next few years, that Galen received what amounted to his most extensive medical training. As physician and surgeon to the gladiators fighting in the arenas, he operated on wounds, set broken bones and supervised his patients' daily diet. It was a crash course in practical anatomy and medicine, and it was during these years that Galen published the first of his many medical treatises.

By the time he moved to Rome, six years later, Galen was already a famous physician. In Rome his reputation increased as he successfully treated many of the city's most respected citizens, including the philosopher Eudemus. Extremely confident of his own abilities, he never discouraged the title "wonder worker" soon applied to him. Nor did he refrain from criticizing what he saw as the ineptitude of many of the city's other leading physicians. The battle became so pitched at one point that Galen was forced by his adversaries to leave Rome. It was a brief exile, however. It ended in triumph for Galen when he was appointed personal physician to the great Stoic emperor, Marcus Aurelius. Back in Rome, safely and profitably practicing his profession among the wealthy and influential dignitaries of the court, he wrote a series of books that profoundly influenced generations of physicians following him.

Galen lived during a time when Christianity was becoming popular and powerful, and although he was not a Christian, he developed a kind of monotheism, believing that everything in the universe was created by God for a particular and specific purpose. He believed the human body and its organization was proof of the power and wisdom of the creator and that it demonstrated the divine design in all things. This teleological belief made his work very popular with the Christian church and helped his books survive through the centuries.

Unfortunately this same teleology, or belief in a grand design or purpose, hampered progress in the fields of biology and medicine for more than a thousand years. As long as such grand designs were believed to be *the reason* certain phenomena existed, the true causes of the phenomena were often misinterpreted, unsought or undiscovered. The brain of a human fetus, for instance, was believed by Galen to be formed at the very last, since it was obvious that the fetus did not *need* a brain until it was ready to be born.

Galen produced a remarkable 256 treatises in all, dealing not only with medicine, but with philosophy, law, grammar and mathematics. The vast majority, however, were on medicine and 15 of those concerned anatomy, his special interest. His most famous book, *On Anatomical Preparations,* remained the standard text for anatomical studies for more than 1,400 years. Unfortunately, as with many of his other medical works, including those containing his beliefs about the movement of blood within the body, this work contained many significant errors. While Galen was an astute and

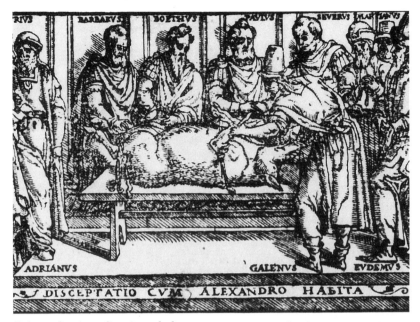

Galen performing a dissection as he lectures   (National Library of Medicine)

careful anatomist, he was forbidden by Roman law to dissect human bodies. So instead he used sheep, oxen, dogs, bears, monkeys and apes, the last of which he believed to be essentially similar to human beings. And all Galen's descriptions of human anatomy were influenced by his close examination, not of humans, but of the animals he was permitted to dissect. Galen himself cautioned against paying too blind an homage to books: "If anyone wishes to observe the works of nature, he should put his trust not in books of anatomy but in his own eyes . . . ," he wrote. Nevertheless, his own books, copied and often miscopied, were passed down through the centuries and became, like Ptolemy's in astronomy, the unquestioned word in the study of medicine and anatomy.

It was this "authority of Galen," and indirectly the authority of Aristotle (whose philosophy Galen had been steeped in), that Andreas Vesalius bumped heads with when he began his medical studies in 1530.

Few others had much influence. Although some useful work had been done in the field of medicine, most notably by two Persians, Rhazes (b. A.D. 852) and Avicenna (b. A.D. 980), both medicine and anatomy had suffered a long decline after the fall of Rome, and throughout the medieval ages. During the great reawakening known as the Renaissance, the famous artist and sculptor Leonardo da Vinci had studied both animal and human anatomy and composed an impressive number of exacting sketches and

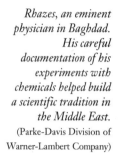

Rhazes, an eminent physician in Baghdad. His careful documentation of his experiments with chemicals helped build a scientific tradition in the Middle East.
(Parke-Davis Division of Warner-Lambert Company)

notes. Leonardo, though, was an artist and not a scientist. And while his work was excellent in many details, the many leaps of his curiosity from subject to subject kept him from applying the full scope of his intellect in one area for very long.

VESALIUS THE ANATOMIST

It was the impatient young physician, Andreas Vesalius (1514–64), who bent to the task of shattering the chains placed by Galen on the understanding of anatomy. Born in Brussels, Belgium into a family of physicians (his grandfather and great-grandfather had been physicians and his father was pharmacist to Charles V), Vesalius [veh-SAY-lee-us] found his vocation early. As a youngster he was already practicing his craft by performing dissections on dogs, cats and other small animals, on his mother's kitchen table. Beginning his medical studies more officially at the age of 16, he spent the next few years studying at the University of Louvain in Belgium, transferring to the University of Paris in 1533. He first studied under and then assisted Jacob Sylvius, who was then the dominant medical figure at the University of Paris, and Vesalius quickly built himself a reputation for quick study, hard work and strong opinions. Those opinions soon caused him to quarrel heatedly with Sylvius. But as he continued work on his own, his reputation was soon so great that the other physicians and students often called upon him to demonstrate his dissecting techniques. The quarrels, however, continued, not just with Sylvius, but with other members of the faculty. The source of most of these arguments was Vesalius's growing disenchantment with the teaching of Galen, whose works were still being taught uncritically in the scholastic tradition.

In the summer of 1536 war broke out between France and the German Empire, and 21-year-old Vesalius, as an enemy alien, was forced to leave Paris and return to Louvain. Since he had been forced from Paris without graduating, he picked up his medical studies immediately upon arriving back at Louvain.

The next few months were the most macabre in Vesalius's medical career. Because students were required to see human dissections, even though such dissections were unpopular with the church and authorities, who strictly regulated the number of corpses available for study, Vesalius became, among other accomplishments, an able grave-robber. On one occasion he even stole the bones of a criminal that had been left rotting and swinging from the gallows, and he hid the disassembled skeleton underneath his bed.

After his second stay at Louvain and a short stint in military service, he moved on to the University of Venice. During his brief visit there he became a lecturer and astounded and enraged many of the faculty by abandoning the standard scholastic practice of merely lecturing from a raised platform while an assistant or lowly barber-surgeon performed the dissection under discussion. The old ways, he cursed, were "detestable procedures," and those that performed them were "jackdaws aloft in their high chairs, with egregious arrogance croaking things that they had never investigated . . ." Taking knife in hand, Vesalius performed the dissection himself, lecturing

Vesalius giving a lecture as he performs a dissection (Parke-Davis, Division of Warner-Lambert Company)

to the assembled students despite the unpleasant stench. In those days before refrigeration, most complete dissections took two or three days, and although they were usually held in the open air, the situation was extremely trying for both students and practitioners.

The next stop for the wandering anatomist was at the famous University of Padua in Italy. There, within two days of his admittance as a graduate student, he was awarded his Doctor of Medicine degree in December 1537 and was appointed to a full professorship. At the age of 23 Andreas Vesalius became a member of the most prestigious medical faculty in Europe.

It was at Padua that Vesalius gave full rein to his disagreement with the teachings of Galen. Since Galen's dissections had been performed upon monkeys and apes rather than humans, it was inevitable that some sharp-eyed anatomist working on humans would discover the errors in Galen's writings. It's even likely that some of those errors were discovered by others before Vesalius made his prolonged attack on the earlier man's authority. A few apologetic anatomists argued that the human body had obviously gone through some changes since the time of Galen's dissections. The thigh bone, for instance, was obviously straight where Galen described it as curved. That might have been caused, according to some of Galen's apologists, by the wearing of the tight trousers that were not worn in Galen's time. These arguments didn't always convince everyone, but for the most part, the doubters remained silent.

It was Vesalius, with his passion for hard work and truth, who finally mounted the attack. Ironically, although his own dissections on the human body had revealed many differences with Galen's text, it was while dissecting a monkey that Vesalius discovered the truth. He found, as he later wrote, "a small projection of bone upon one vertebra of its spine." Galen had described this feature many times when writing of human anatomy, but Vesalius had never seen it in his own dissections on humans. The answer was immediately obvious. Galen had not dissected humans but monkeys. The standard text on human anatomy was not describing humans at all but was a clever embellishment and projection of the actual anatomy of a monkey to the supposed anatomy of a human.

Once he had publicly stated his belief that Galen had never worked on human dissections at all, Vesalius began a full-scale assault upon Galen's text as a final authority. While not personally faulting Galen as a physician— after all, he had done the best that he could under the circumstances—the fact was, Vesalius argued, that there were just too many differences between monkeys and humans for the anatomy of one to be used as a map for the anatomy of the other.

At Padua, Vesalius graphically illustrated this point by arranging a dramatic demonstration. Displaying two skeletons side by side, one an ape's and the other a human's, he was able to point out more than 200 differences between the ape and human skeletons alone. The appendage Galen had described as extending from the vertebra, he showed, appeared only on the ape's skeleton. On the human skeleton, there was none.

Controversy swirled around him, since most of the physicians at Padua still defended the sanctity of Galenic thought, and Vesalius's lectures became among the most popular and lively at the school. Still shocking many by taking the knife in hand himself, he had increased the time spent for each dissection from three days to three weeks, taking special and thorough care with each part of his dissection and lecture. To minimize the obvious problems of the body's decay, the dissections were held in the winter and several different bodies were used at one time so that different parts could be compared and contrasted.

He wanted to reach a wider audience than his classrooms and public lectures, so in 1543 Vesalius published his famous book *De humani corporis fabrica*. It was a landmark event—so much so that today the field of anatomy is generally thought of in three phases, the pre-Vesalian, the Vesalian and the post-Vesalian periods.

The *Fabrica* was the most accurate book on human anatomy up to that time, and today it is still astounding in its accuracy and beauty. Composed with the same kind of careful exactness that Vesalius had demonstrated in his lectures, the *Fabrica* also benefited greatly from the outstanding illustrations prepared by Vesalius and Jan Stephen van Calcar, a pupil of the great Venetian artist Titian (c. 1490–1576). The human body was shown in its natural positions, and many of the muscles and organs were executed so exactly that they are the equal of many of today's finest and most expensive textbook illustrations. Thanks also to the perfection of the printing press in the 14th–15th centuries, both the text and illustrations could be reproduced exactly without the many errors, especially in the illustrations, that would have resulted if the books had been copied by hand in the ancient ways. For the printing job, Vesalius, sparing no expense, selected Johannes Oporinus, a famous printer from Basel who was esteemed for his meticulousness.

As excellent as the *Fabrica* was in many ways, today's medical student would be quick to spot its numerous errors and deficiencies. Although his ideas about anatomy were amazingly accurate, Vesalius was still a student of Galen in many areas. His physiology (whereas anatomy deals with the structure of living organisms, physiology deals with their functioning) was still steeped in ancient traditions. He believed, for instance, that the act of digestion was accomplished by some kind of "cooking" of the food in the abdominal cavity and that respiration was for "cooling the blood." He also initially accepted Galen's views on the heart and circulatory system, believing that blood must pass through invisible pores from one side of the heart to the other. However, later in life he began to change his mind based on the evidence.

Drawing of the human muscle system from the Fabrica *by Vesalius*
(Courtesy California State University at Sacramento Library)

Despite these deficiencies, now known, the *Fabrica* was a deserved success. Many copies were "pirated"; that is, the text and illustrations were plagiarized and reprinted without his permission. This practice persisted during his lifetime and long after his death.

Curiously, the *Fabrica* was Vesalius's final lecture. Perhaps he was worn out by the storm of protest issuing from the defenders of the Galenic tradition, or perhaps he believed that he had completed the work he was destined to accomplish. Shortly after the book's publication he abandoned the teaching of anatomy and secured a position as physician to Charles V and later Charles's son, the Spanish king, Philip the Second. When he was returning from a pilgrimage, his ship was badly damaged by a storm off the coast of Greece, and he died shortly after managing to reach the island of Zanti in October 1564.

THE SEEDS OF CHANGE

Vesalius had struck a major but not final blow to the "Tyranny of Galen." Although many were converted by Vesalius's convincing and eloquent arguments, many others remained bound in the Galenic tradition. Despite Vesalius's teaching, the University of Padua, for instance, remained a Galenic and Aristotelian stronghold for many years to come. Still, the first chink in the Galenic armor had been discovered, and many of Vesalius's contemporaries and followers began to strike quietly out on their own toward new discoveries.

One of the more interesting of those was the French surgeon Ambroise Paré (1510–90). The son of a barber-surgeon, Paré entered the trade at an early age. The position was a lowly one. The services of surgeons were generally confined to court nobility, high clergy and wealthy merchants; other patients were left to the care of barber-surgeons, who combined their daily routine of cutting hair with their surgical business. This usually

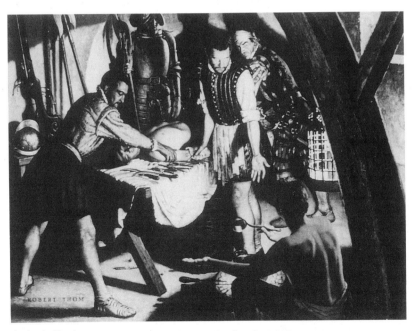

Ambroise Paré (Parke-Davis, Division of Warner-Lambert Company)

involved such procedures as blood-letting, lancing boils, pulling teeth and opening up abscesses, but many of the barber-surgeons also performed amputations and other operations when needed. Given the general incompetence and ineptitude of many of these ill-trained barber-surgeons, the trade was greatly looked down upon by the better educated and more qualified surgeons and physicians.

Paré, who was gifted with a quick mind and agile hands, decided that his best opportunity would come from employing his talent in the service of the military. For the next 30 years, he served with the French army in its protracted wars with Italy. Participating in 20 campaigns, Paré also found time to publish 20 books that profoundly influenced the advancement of surgery. In them he attacked such practices as the use of boiling oil in the treatment of gunshot wounds. He championed the use of tying bleeding vessels with a ligature rather than cauterizing them (burning them shut with a hot iron or chemical) as was the standard practice at the time. Although he was snubbed by the more "learned" medical men for the practice of writing in French rather than Latin, Paré also wrote summaries of the works of Vesalius, in an attempt to bring Vesalius's teaching to the hands of his fellow barber-surgeons.

Vesalius's teaching position at the University of Padua meanwhile had fallen into the hands of one of his students Gabriel Fallopius (1523–62). Rising eventually to the rank of full professor, Fallopius is best known today for his careful descriptions of the inner ear and of the organs of reproduction. He was the discoverer of the Fallopian tubes, although he didn't understand their function. Fallopius also invented the condom. Fallopius's successor at Padua was one of *his* ex-students, the anatomist Hieronymus Fabricius (1537–1619). Among other things, Fabricius [fah-BRISH-us] is generally credited with the first accurate description of the valves in the veins. He was also a teacher of William Harvey (see Chapter Eight).

Although the anatomists were slowly making discoveries, like explorers beginning to chart the interior of the human body, anatomy itself could not solve the mysteries of function. What did those parts truly do in relation to the whole? And how did they do it? Fabricius, for instance, thought that the valves in the veins served as some kind of floodgates that controlled how much blood was allowed to flow to different parts of the body. Their true function as regulators for the one-way direction of blood flow would only be understood once people comprehended how the heart and circulatory system functioned. For a full understanding of the human body and the way that it worked, much more needed to be learned. New theories had to be developed. But the answers could not come from anatomy alone. Progress in many other areas needed to be made.

PARACELSUS, PHARMACEUTICALS AND MEDICINE

*P*hilippus Aureolus Theophrastus Bombastus von Hohenheim—the name is a mouthful. History knows him as Paracelsus, and he was one of the strangest characters of the 16th century. Was he an alchemist, a charlatan, a mystic, a crank? Was he a physician, a medical reformer, a crusader, a teacher? He was all of these at the same time. There is no mystery to Paracelsus, no going back to try and find the truth, no final resolution. You take him as you find him, a tumultuous bundle of contradictions, a genius, a crank, a con man, a humanitarian.

By the 16th century, alchemy had traveled a long and for the most part unswerving road since its early beginnings in ancient China and Egypt. Its major objective, to transform base metals into gold, remained unchanged, but other, more mystical objectives also motivated the quest. For many the power achieved by discovering the means to create the purity of gold would also confer upon its discoverer the elixir of life, thus ensuring personal sanctity and immortality. The alchemists' quest during the 16th century was for the "philosopher's stone," the secret key that would bring to the discoverer the ultimate in both physical and spiritual wealth.

Bent over the tools and apparatus of their trade—the open fire, elaborately shaped glass containers, melting pots, measuring devices, mortars and pestles—many of the alchemists were strange and driven men. With so much at stake, such high desires, with success perhaps only a slight change in experiment away (an extra drop of mercury perhaps, a dash of this, a dash of that, a slightly longer melting time), it was little wonder that they often appeared strange. After all, it was a basic belief of alchemy that the act itself, the experiment, the search, would change the character of the man.

An alchemist at work (National Library of Medicine)

The changes were not always for the better. For many the relentless quest for the archaic and secret knowledge that they believed lay in the philosopher's stone branched off into other strange directions. Most alchemists believed in astrology and other magic and mystic arts. Many were numerologists, believing in the secret divining power of numbers. Many more searched out the "truth" to be found in black magic and occult practices. Not a few were accused by the religious of making pacts with the devil. Some thought that perhaps they could make such a pact—if only they could discover the right incantation to call up the evil old fellow. Failing that, certainly they could at least summon forth some lesser demons to do their bidding.

Still others, needing to finance their research, or finding themselves desperately trying to secure their reputations as miracle workers, turned to outright fraud and chicanery. Elaborate confidence tricks were devised to fool the unsuspecting into thinking that the perpetrator had already discovered the secret of turning metal into gold or had some other occult powers. Sometimes this cheating was rationalized by the alchemist as necessary, until he could discover the real secret. Sometimes the cheating was just an easy way to make quick money from the gullible.

PARACELSUS, THE PHYSICIAN

Paracelsus [par-ah-SEL-sus] was born in eastern Switzerland in 1493. His father was a physician, the illegitimate son of a noble family. His mother was a bondswoman of a Benedictine Abbey near Einsiedeln. Little else is known about his childhood. His mother was apparently of somewhat unstable mind and died, perhaps by suicide, when Paracelsus was nine. Some rumors have said that Paracelsus also was the illegitimate son of a noble family, and was "adopted" in turn by *his* father.

Little more is known about where he picked up his medical knowledge. He began his long life of wandering at the age of 14 and may have spent a brief period at the University of Basel when he was 16. Some sources say that for a brief period he was also a student of Bishop Trithemius at

Paracelsus, who broke with Galen's physiology, also claimed to have the "secret of immortality" hidden in the head of his cane.
(National Library of Medicine)

Würzburg. Although he practiced medicine for the rest of his life, there is no evidence that he ever actually received a medical diploma.

We do know that his first "official" practice as a physician was at the famous Fugger mines in the Tyrol. It may have been there that he picked up his consuming interest in alchemy. Sigismund Fugger, one of the owners of the mines, was a devout alchemist, and the location was an ideal one in which to experiment with various metals. It was also at the Fugger mines that Paracelsus began to develop some of his controversial medical theories.

According to the traditional teachings of Galen, which were in turn greatly influenced by the philosophy of Aristotle, all illnesses suffered by the human body were a result of an imbalance in the body's four "humors." Those humors, according to the ancients, were blood, phlegm, choler and melancholy (black choler). Each individual's body contained a unique balance of these humors. The dominance of one or another of these substances also determined the unique nature of the individual. Thus, a person whose nature was sad or melancholic was thought to have a high amount of melancholy in his or her system. It was the person's unique natural state, distinguishing him or her from the rest. Disease occurred when that natural state was disrupted by the development of more or less than the person's normal amount of one or another of the four humors. It was up to the physician to discover the unique natural balance within each patient and restore that balance through such means as blood-letting, purging, sweating or forced vomiting.

While working among the miners and metal workers, Paracelsus treated the frequent occupational hazard of lung disease, and, through observation, came to some different conclusions. He soon came to believe that the cause of the body's disorder was not some internal imbalance of imaginary humors, which he ridiculed as absurd and archaic. Instead he thought disease resulted from some *external* cause. He reasoned that, in the case of the miners, lung disease was probably caused by something breathed in through the air or absorbed by contact through the skin. It was an important insight, and one that would later help him form the basis of his theory that many diseases sprang from "seeds," one of the earliest versions of germ theory. With his growing belief that life was a chemical process and disease was a defect in the body's chemistry, he began to think in terms of using alchemy to create chemicals that could restore the body's health. He wrote the first book on miners' diseases, and his research led him to introduce various combinations of lead, sulfur, iron, copper sulfate, arsenic and potassium sulfate into medical practice. He also experimented with ether as an anesthetic, trying it out on chickens, although its general use on human beings would not come into practice until many years later.

PARACELSUS, THE ALCHEMIST

A contemporary of Paracelsus, the German mineralogist Georgius Agricola, was working along similar lines. This "iatrochemistry," as chemistry in the service of medicine has come to be called, marked an important beginning—the attempt to treat disease through chemistry and new inorganic drugs. It was a far cry from the simple organic herbal remedies employed by the ancients and still championed by many today.

Unfortunately, Paracelsus was still an alchemist at heart and still deeply immersed in the magic and superstition of the alchemist's art. His belief in astrology, for instance, had led him to believe that different parts of the human body were governed by the planets. The heart, he thought, was subject to the influence of the Sun, the brain subject to the position of the Moon, and the liver, to the influence of Jupiter. He had also come to the mystical conclusion, not only that the physiological processes of the body were chemical transformations, but that those transformations were governed by a mysterious spiritual entity called the "archeus." The archeus, according to his theory, resided in the stomach. Death resulted when this entity either died or was lost. In the treatment of wounds he still believed in the ancient superstition of "weapon-salve," in which a salve was applied to the instrument causing the wound, rather than to the wound itself! The healing, according to ancient belief, would be caused by the sympathetic power transmitted from the blood on the weapon to the blood of the afflicted. He also claimed to have created a homunculus, a tiny, perfectly formed human, which he had incubated inside a gourd without the help of any woman!

Little wonder, with this strange hodgepodge of ideas, that Paracelsus was and still remains such a controversial figure. After moving from the Fugger

Paracelsus at work in his laboratory
(Parke-Davis, Division of Warner-Lambert Company)

95

SANCTORIUS (SANTORIO SANTORIO)

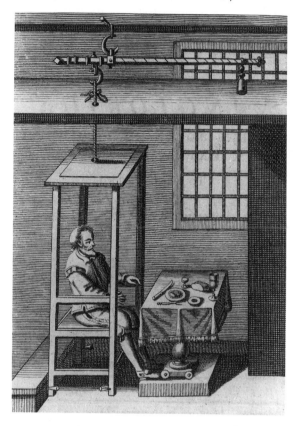

*Sanctorius in his
weighing chair*
(National Library of
Medicine)

mines, his career as an alchemist and physician was a roller-coaster ride of ups and downs. His personality, as erratic as his ideas, did not help matters. Egocentric to the point of swaggering absurdity, he was also a heavy drinker with a dangerous temper. He was a dandy given to living an outlandish life-style when he had the money, and he was also a chronic complainer and paranoid, given to blaming all his problems on the dishonesty and stupidity of others when the money ran out. It was not a reputation to inspire confidence in a physician.

For a while he apparently enjoyed a brief spell of success as a practicing physician in Strasbourg, enough so that he was invited to the University of Basel to fill an open teaching position. There he angered other physicians

A friend of Galileo, Sanctorius (1561–1636) graduated from the University of Padua in medicine in 1587. After practicing medicine in Venice for a few years, he was appointed physician to the king of Poland. Fourteen years later he resumed his medical practice in Venice. He was appointed to the chair of theoretical medicine at Padua in 1611, and he resigned in 1629 to again practice private medicine and continue his research.

Sanctorius's research was devoted to his pioneering work in a field he called Medical Statics. Influenced by Galileo's quantitative experiments, Sanctorius founded the modern study of metabolism (the transformations that make up the life processes). Of course, Sanctorius didn't know that was what he was doing. He was a Galenist and tried to understand the exact balance of the four humors in the body. To do this Sanctorius decided to measure everything that went into his body as well as everything that came out of it. For the best part of 30 years he spent as many hours as he could in his specially devised "weighing chair." Noticing that less weight came out of his body than went in, he devised a theory of "insensible perspiration," a process that he thought accounted for the missing amount. His theories were popular for a while, although they were in error, but, more important, he pioneered the idea of taking and keeping exacting measurement of the body's processes. He invented an awkward but usable thermometer for measuring body temperature, an instrument for measuring humidity and a special bed by which patients could be cooled or heated in water. He also developed a means by which pulses could be measured, using a simple string pendulum in which the string could be lengthened or shortened to match the beat of the pulse. By comparing the lengths of strings he could then measure variations of the pulse beats.

by first refusing to take the Hippocratic Oath—which is administered to all physicians even up to this day—and then by publicly burning the books of Galen, proclaiming with typical grandiloquence "My beard knows more than you and your writers." It was not a performance to endear him to many people, particularly since rumor has it that he was drunk at the time.

Paracelsus was asked to leave Basel after a stormy two years, and he spent the rest of his life more or less on the run. Moving from city to city, he continued his attacks on Galen and the ancient theory of humors. He also attacked and angered the local physicians for what he saw as the deficiencies and ignorance of their medical treatments. Practicing his own bizarre blend of mysticism, alchemy and medicine, he was for the rest of his life always a

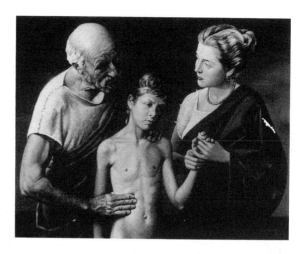

*Hippocrates (460
B.C.–370 B.C.) was
regarded as a great
physician in his lifetime
and established the
Hippocratic Oath,
which physicians still
adhere to today.*
(Parke-Davis, Division of
Warner-Lambert Company)

figure of controversy, battle and retreat. Each short period of success, it seemed, was destined for failure, and his temperament became more and more strange. He claimed that he had demons at his command that would destroy all his adversaries at his will, and that he had discovered the alchemist's long-sought-after "secret to immortality," which was hidden in the fancy head of his cane.

How much of this nonsense Paracelsus actually believed and how much was sham and bombast we will never know. The last years of his life were filled with poverty and drunken despair. He died on September 24, 1541, in the city of Salzburg. Some said that he was murdered by his enemies. Others that he died in a drunken accident.

How much this strange man contributed to the history of science is still controversial. Certainly others, such as his contemporary Agricola, had also begun to pursue the ideas of a chemical understanding of the body and the chemical treatment of disease. Johann Baptista van Helmont (1579–1644), the Flemish physician and alchemist, and Franciscus Sylvius (1614–72), the Dutch physician, would each in his own way advance the understanding of chemistry and medicine. But none in his time was more outspoken and courageous in the defense of this revolutionary idea than the flamboyant Paracelsus. His defiance of the traditional and stagnant views of Galen and his concept of the life processes as chemical processes would help to open a new phase in the early history of physiology. Others, such as Sanctorius (see box), began to pursue the sideroads of physiology created by the new approach established by iatrochemistry. Paracelsus and other iatrochemists had opened a new avenue of research into the exploration of life science, and for his contribution to this important advancement alone he deserves our recognition.

THE HEART OF THE MATTER: WILLIAM HARVEY AND THE CIRCULATION OF THE BLOOD

Although Vesalius had begun to challenge the strong hold that Galenic theory held on anatomy, and Paracelsus and others were attempting to weaken Galen's grip on the practice of medicine, physiology in the 17th century was still stifled by the ancient ideas.

To understand the physiology of the human body, how its various parts functioned (what their jobs were and how they did them), it was crucial to understand the heart and blood. The hero of this part of our story was a mild-mannered English physician named William Harvey.

BEFORE HARVEY: EARLY IDEAS ABOUT BLOOD

Long before Galen's time, blood was recognized for its special importance to the human body. Even the most primitive societies endowed it with special qualities, and today we still speak of blood bonds, blood oaths. "You can't squeeze blood from a turnip," we say. Enemies are said to have "bad blood" between them. The ruthless rival is "cold blooded." In some societies blood was used to seal wedding and business contracts. Some ancient tribes believed that drinking blood would give courage and youth. And the legend of the vampire, endlessly seeking the blood of others to assure its own immortality, persists in popular culture. Many poorly informed people still believe today that a blood transfusion may pass personality traits from the donor to the receiver.

Both Hippocrates and Aristotle knew that the movement of the blood within the body was basic to the process of life.

Aristotle's studies had led him to the conclusion that the heart was the central organ of the body. It was, according to Aristotle, the seat of intelligence. It also controlled the flow of the blood and supplied the blood with its animal heat.

Galen, after extensively gathering together all that the ancients understood about blood and completing his own experiments, came to a different and much more elaborate conclusion. He believed the body was governed physiologically by three distinct sets of organs, fluids and spirits. The three seats of these systems were the liver, the heart and the brain.

All blood, according to Galen's theory, originated in the liver. Food taken in by the body was "boiled" or "cooked" within the stomach, where it was converted to a fluid substance called *chyle*. The chyle moved to the liver where it was converted into blood and infused with "natural spirits," which governed nutrition. The liver was the beginning, the fountainhead so to speak, of all the veins. Through the network of veins, like an internal irrigation system, the entire body was furnished with blood, dark red with the nutrients and "natural spirits" it contained. Each part of the body attracted to itself the blood it needed, which arrived through a sort of ebb and flow.

Reaching the right side of the heart through the veins, some blood passed, Galen thought, from the right side of the heart to the left through tiny invisible pores in the septum (the partition between the two sides). On the right side of the heart this blood was mixed with air drawn into the heart from the lungs; it became charged with "vital spirits," which governed the passions, and the blood, now a much brighter red, proceeded to the rest of the body through the system of arteries.

Some of this arterial blood went to the brain, where "animal spirits" were manufactured and distributed to the body through the nervous system, which Galen thought was a network of hollow tubes. The "animal spirits" governed sensation and motion.

In Galen's view then the primary importance of the blood was to distribute the important "vital spirits." The "spirits" themselves caused the blood to move. The lung's function was to cool and ventilate the innately hot heart—hot because it was the seat of the "soul." And the heart he believed to be primarily concerned with preparing the "vital spirits" and sucking in air during its active stage, called systole, and allowing it to drain off during diastole.

Like most of Galen's theories, the whole system, with its various mystical infusions of governing "spirits," its correspondences with theological thinking, and its elaborate internal consistency, had a great appeal to many Christians. By the 16th century, though, it had begun to develop some holes.

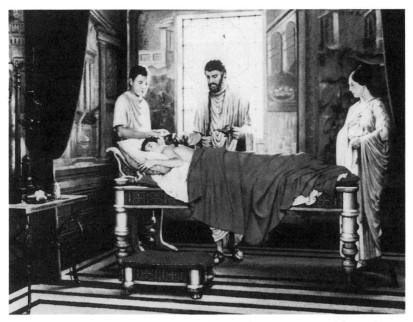

Although he was one of the great physicians of all time, Galen nonetheless left a misleading legacy of ideas about blood and its distribution in the body. (Parke-Davis, Division of Warner-Lambert Company)

Or more specifically, some anatomists were having trouble finding some very important holes: the tiny pores, or passages, in the septum between the two sides of the heart.

Michael Servetus (c. 1511–53), a controversial and outspoken Spanish physician, was one of the first to come to the conclusion that the passages did not exist. His studies of Galen and other anatomists, as well as his own direct observations, had led him to form an alternative theory about the movement of the blood within the body. If the passages did not exist, Servetus [sur-VEE-tus] reasoned, then not much blood could move from the right to the left side of the heart. Noting that the pulmonary artery was quite large and that blood moved very forcefully from the heart to the lungs, he reasoned that more blood was being sent to the lungs than was necessary just for their nourishment. The blood must move to the lungs for aeration, he argued, and it was during its passage through the lungs that the color changed. Afterward it was returned through the pulmonary vein. At no time, he argued, did it actually pass through the heart muscle. Servetus was not a well known anatomist, or even much of a physician, but his idea of this "lesser circulation" may have encouraged more people to challenge Galen's intellectual and philosophical lock on physiology.

Unfortunately, given the unsettled religious temper of his day, Servetus was as outspoken as a theologian as he was as a physician. His heretical religious views managed to make him powerful enemies, not only among the Catholics, but among the Protestants as well. Not one to easily accept censure, he pushed his luck too far. Both the Catholic church and the Protestants angrily called for his immediate execution. Managing to escape the clutches of the Catholic Inquisition, he was captured by the Protestants in Geneva. There, under the direct orders of John Calvin, he was bound with an iron chain and burned alive at the stake—having been denied the "mercy" of first being strangled.

The challenge to Galen, however, continued. Another more famous anatomist was also bothered by not being able to discover the tiny passages, so important to Galen's theory. "The septum is as thick, dense, and compact as the rest of the heart. I do not see therefore, how even the smallest particle can be transferred from the right to the left ventricle through it," wrote Andreas Vesalius in 1555. Still very much a Galenist when it came to physiology, Vesalius assumed that the pores must exist but that they were much too tiny to ever be discovered.

"The movements of the heart are known to God alone," wrote one of Vesalius's bewildered contemporaries.

One of Vesalius's students, Realdo Columbo (1516–59), was also one of his most outspoken critics. Succeeding Vesalius as professor of surgery and anatomy at Padua, Columbo was one of the most vocal attackers of the *Fabrica*. While his personal and professional reputation apparently left much to be desired, he did write a medical treatise, *De re anatomica* ("On Anatomy"), which was published by his children in 1559. Although some of its critics called it a pale imitation of the *Fabrica* (but without illustrations), it did contain Columbo's theories about the movement of the blood within the body. Columbo's arguments, that the blood flowed from the right to the left side of the heart through the lungs, may have been borrowed from his reading of Servetus, but they were clearly written and represent the first publication of this idea of the so-called lesser circulation by a well-known anatomist. The work, however, did not spark a major revolution against Galen's well-entrenched ideas about the heart and blood. Columbo's reputation was not solid enough, nor was his "evidence" strong enough, to allow many people to take his ideas seriously. The solution to the problems of the heart and blood, and the real revolution against Galen's physiology, would wait another seven decades until a gifted and dedicated English physician would finally lay the problem to rest.

Like another great scientist, Charles Darwin, whom we will meet in another volume in this series, William Harvey was a reluctant revolutionary. A quiet, decent and conservative man who revered both Galen and Aristotle,

Harvey developed theories and careful proof of the circulation of blood that would deal the last major blow to Galenic medicine.

BIG IDEAS IN A SMALL BOOK

William Harvey was born in Folkestone, on the south coast of England, on April 1, 1578. His father was a prosperous farmer who later moved into commerce and eventually became mayor of Folkestone. Like his six brothers, Harvey enjoyed a comfortable life and benefited from remarkably close-knit family bonds. Although William was the only one of his father's sons to go into the academic life (all six of the others became prosperous merchants), all the brothers remained close. Of his two sisters, one died at an early age and little is known of the other, but his brothers all lived and thrived into old age, often aiding each other financially and emotionally. It was a warm and secure childhood and probably contributed later to William Harvey's sense of modest self-assurance.

At the age of 10 William entered the King's School, Canterbury, and he went from there to Cambridge University with a medical scholarship in 1593. Even as a child he displayed a keen interest in medicine, and, like Vesalius, he dissected small animals in the family kitchen. He also studied the hearts of animals given to him by the local butchers and a nearby slaughterhouse.

Harvey received his Bachelor of Arts degree from Caius College, Cambridge in 1597, and in 1599 he journeyed to the best place in the world for a young medical student to study: the famous University of Padua in Italy. There he became a student of the renowned Fabricius, who had recently built Padua's first indoor amphitheater devoted solely to performing dissections. Ranking second only to Vesalius as the period's greatest anatomist, Fabricius, who in 1603 published his discovery of the valves in the veins, became a major influence on the 21-year-old Harvey. Harvey served as Fabricus's special assistant, and he developed a close association with the "master." It was at Padua that Harvey picked up his life-long habit of wearing a small silver dagger hung from his waist. It was also at Padua that he may have begun his addiction to coffee, which was then a much rarer beverage than it is today. Many historians, noting comments from Harvey's contemporaries about his surprisingly quick temper, irritability and frequent attacks of insomnia, credit his coffee-drinking habits for these phenomena in the normally easygoing physician.

More important, though, it was at Padua that Harvey became seriously interested in the problems of the heart and blood movement.

Although Fabricius didn't publish his ideas about the valves in the veins until 1603, Harvey had certainly learned about them early in his work with Fabricius. His time studying under Fabricius, as well as attending anatomy lectures in the amphitheater, stirred his mind. Late in his life he wrote to British physicist and chemist Robert Boyle that it was the valves in the veins that got him to thinking about the possible one-way flow of blood within the body. So did a dramatic incident when a friend of Harvey's suffered a severed artery in his arm during a knife fight in the always rowdy atmosphere of Padua. Watching the treatment of the wound, Harvey noted that the blood came rushing out in spurts, quite differently than the way it drained smoothly from the veins. It looked to the young Harvey almost as if it were being pumped.

His professors had taught him also that there were two basically different kinds of blood in the body: one being the blood from the liver, which supplied the nourishment, or "animal spirits," and the other being the blood from the heart, which furnished the "vital spirits," including heat and energy. Despite the color differences, the blood appeared much the same to the inquisitive Harvey. He tasted it and it even tasted the same. Maybe it was the same. If that were so, he began to wonder, then maybe only one kind of blood circulated throughout the entire body. And maybe it was actually pumped by the heart. It was the beginning of an idea, and it certainly fit in with his Aristotelian philosophy.

Although the great Galileo was teaching at Padua while Harvey was a student there, the university remained solidly pro-Ptolemaic in astronomy and solidly Galenic in most of its medicine. Aristotle had taught the perfection and beauty of circles. "I began to think whether there might not be a motion as it were in a circle," Harvey later wrote, "in the same way as Aristotle says that the air and the rain emulate the circular motion of the superior bodies."

Cautious and conservative, he did not press his ideas at Padua. Ideas were not proofs. He received his Doctor of Medicine degree in 1602 and returned to England to begin his practice of medicine. There he married the daughter of a prominent physician and rose rapidly in his career, becoming in succession fellow of the College of Physicians, physician to St. Bartholomew's Hospital, professor of anatomy at the College of Physicians and Surgeons and physician extraordinary to James I and Charles I. Harvey also remained a close personal friend and confidant to Charles throughout that sovereign's troubled career.

Throughout his extraordinary rise in social and medical prestige, he remained always a dedicated pursuer of knowledge. And, if his unremarkable medical practice earned him a reputation for being a somewhat mediocre practitioner (he was still very much under the influence of Galen in his treatment of various day-to-day medical problems), his dedication to understanding the working of the human body led him to perform autopsies on close friends and even on his own father and sister.

By 1616, his lecture notes indicate that he was already on his way to arriving at his understanding of the circulation of blood within the body. His revolutionary work *Exercitatio anatomica de motu cordis et sanguinis in animalibus* ("On the Movement of the Heart and Blood in Animals") was published 12 years later, and remains one of the great early masterpieces in science. If Harvey was Aristotelian and traditionalist in his philosophy, he was modern in his experimental and research techniques.

For Harvey the matter was one of fluid mechanics. He isolated the problem and refused to try to draw grand schemes about nature in general. How the blood flows, and what part the heart plays in its motion, were his primary concerns. He did not concern himself with the mysterious "spirits" in *De Motu Cordis*, explaining, "Whether or not the heart, besides propelling the blood, giving it motion locally, and distributing it to the body, adds anything else to it—heat, spirit, perfection—must be inquired into by and by, and decided upon other grounds." Although Harvey philosophically and temperamentally was an old-fashioned Aristotelian, in the spirit of Galileo

William Harvey demonstrating his ideas about blood flow (Parke-Davis, Division of Warner-Lambert Company)

and his times Harvey approached the body as a mechanism and considered it his job to understand the mechanics of the heart and blood.

Like Galileo, too, his approach was carefully and painstakingly experimental. "I do not profess to learn and teach Anatomy from the axioms of

HARVEY AND THE GENERATION OF ANIMALS

Not all of William Harvey's work was devoted to the problems of the circulation of the blood. He was also interested in the problems of animal reproduction. One of the first to study the development of chicks in eggs, he published his results in 1651 in a large book called *De generatione animalium* ("On the Reproduction of Animals"). Working without the aid of a microscope, he examined the development of chicks by carefully opening a different egg in a clutch each day. Noticing that the earliest form appeared to grow from a tiny scab, barely visible to the naked eye (the first appearance of the embryo visible without instruments), he searched for something comparable in mammals. His conclusion was that all creatures must grow from a simple, undifferentiated point of blood, which he called the "primordium." Trying to follow the future developments of the chicks inside the egg, he argued that the embryo develops its future parts slowly as it grows in a process he called "epigenesis." But his work in this field did not win as much acceptance as did his careful research into the circulation of the blood. The book, unfortunately, was also burdened with a general and somewhat heavy-handed Aristotelian philosophy that he had, for the most part, excluded from his great work on circulation.

Instead of Harvey's epigenesis, another, more ancient view soon came to the forefront. Other researchers had arrived at the mistaken conclusion that the embryo was completely formed in its entirety with all of its parts already existing in miniature form within the egg. Within that embryo was another egg and another miniature embryo already formed inside it, and within that, another, and then another, all nested one inside the other like Chinese boxes. Each one was progressively smaller and smaller until they were totally invisible even under the most powerful microscopes of the day. This idea, called "preformation," went as far back as Plato and his idea of perfect forms, and it was endorsed by the church. Even the great microscopist Marcello Malpighi became convinced by his studies that some kind of preformation must take place. This view, and variations on it, would prevail until the late 18th century, when the work of Kaspar Friedrich Wolff and others would throw new light on the problem.

the Philosophers," He wrote in his introduction, "but from Dissections and the Fabrick of Nature."

He began his arguments with evidence drawn from his extensive dissection and vivisection (live dissection) of animals. He carefully discussed the structure of the valves in the heart, the structure of the great vessels and the absence of pores or passages in the septum. None of this made sense, he explained, if one adhered to the traditional views of the movement of the blood according to Galen.

Looking at the problem mechanistically, Harvey argued, one could see that the heart was simply a muscle and that it acted by contracting, pushing blood out. Pointing out that the valves separating the two upper chambers of the heart (the auricles) from the two lower chambers (the ventricles) were one-way, he demonstrated that blood could only flow one way, from auricle to ventricle, and not the other way around. Correctly interpreting the valves in the veins that Fabricius had written about, Harvey pointed out *their* function in also controlling the *direction* of blood flow, and not simply the volume of blood that flowed as Fabricius had thought. The valves in the veins allowed the blood to flow only from the veins to the heart, while the valves in the heart allowed the blood to pass only into the arteries.

Next, he presented some basic mathematical arguments. He calculated that in one hour the heart pumped out an amount of blood that was three times the entire weight of a man! It was unimaginable that in such a short time so much blood could be created at the ends of the veins and destroyed at the ends of the arteries as was demanded in Galen's system. It had to be the same blood, he argued, moving in continuous circulation from the heart to the arteries, from these back to the veins, and then back to the heart.

He also explained how his experiments with snakes had shown that ligation (tying off) of the vena cava (the large vein running into the heart) left the heart empty, while a similar ligation of the aorta (the large artery carrying blood away from the heart) found the blood accumulating in the heart. It was another strong argument in favor of the one-way direction of the bloodstream. He also demonstrated that if an artery was tied off it was the side toward the heart that bulged with blood, while tying off a vein resulted in a bulging on the side away from the heart.

He further drew an example from the practice of blood-letting, demonstrating that a tight application of the bandage compressed the artery and stopped the pulse while looser bandaging produced a slowed flow in the veins. Furthermore, a vein that was emptied between two valves did not refill from above—yet another indication of its one-way movement.

Other examples and experiments further tightened his case. The movement of the blood, he concluded, was a closed circle. It circulated. And the heart was a muscle, a pump that received blood through the veins and pumped it through the arteries by alternate dilation and contraction.

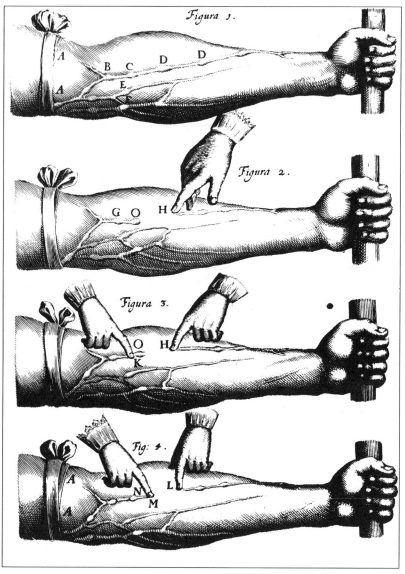

In these drawings from his book, Harvey illustrated his experiment demonstrating that blood flows only one way in the veins: toward the heart. (National Library of Medicine)

In his own words, "the blood in the animal's body is impelled in a circle, and is in a state of ceaseless motion; that is the act or function which the heart performs by means of its pulse; and that is the sole and only end of the motion and contraction of the heart."

It was a well crafted, well proved argument. And his book, despite its slim size (only 72 pages) and terrible production (it was badly printed on cheap paper with many typographical errors) immediately made many converts. For many working physicians it instantly explained among other things how infections, poisons or the venom from snake bites could spread so rapidly throughout the entire system. It also quickly opened up the possibility of injecting medicine directly into the veins to be distributed throughout the entire body. It even inspired some early but largely unsuccessful (since nothing was yet known about different blood types) attempts at blood transfusions.

There were hold-outs; tradition dies hard. And Harvey was one of the first to complain that no one over 30 would understand his work. But his carefully collected evidence—and the work of those following in his foot-steps, particularly Marcello Malpighi, whom we will meet in Chapter 9 and who closed the final gap in Harvey's arguments—eventually won the day.

Unlike Galileo, who had attacked the ancients and scholastics but failed to see his views win wide acceptance, Harvey was much more fortunate. Except for some isolated circumstances, most notably the more conservative

BLOOD AND AIR

William Harvey successfully demonstrated the circulation of the blood, but he offered no complete explanation about the purpose it served within the body. This was left for four other leading experimenters of the 17th century, who arrived at the answer by their cumulative experiments.

Robert Boyle (1627–91) took the first step when he proved by experiments with an air pump that a mouse or bird couldn't live without air. Robert Hooke (1635–1703), who worked for a while as Boyle's assistant before going on to an illustrious career on his own, ran experiments in which he immobilized a dog's lungs but kept the dog alive by blowing air into them. In these experiments, in which he made some of the first demonstrations of artificial respiration, Hooke also showed that it was the air in the blood rather than the actual movements of the lungs that was important for life to continue. The experiments of Richard Lower (1631–91) revealed that dark venous blood became transformed into bright red arterial blood when it passed through the lungs, suggesting to him that something in the air was responsible for the change. And, finally, John Mayow (1643–91) identified this substance in the blood as *spiritus nitro aerus,* or oxygen, as it later would be called, investigated further by the chemist Joseph Priestley over a century later.

medical faculties in France, his work was almost universally accepted by the time of his death in 1657.

It was the last major blow to Galen and the stranglehold that the ancients held upon medicine. The foundations of Galen's thought, weakened tremendously by Vesalius, Harvey and others, were slowly crumbling. With Harvey's work, a new starting point for animal physiology had begun. And more important, perhaps, a major step along the road to the modern experimental approach to the problems in biology had been taken.

"If anyone wishes to observe the works of nature, he should put his trust not in books of anatomy but in his own eyes," Galen himself had written. They were words that the scholastics had not heeded. Perhaps it was right then that the quiet and conservative Harvey had in his own way, by following Galen's own wisdom, paid homage to the ancients he loved so well.

LOOKING AT THE VERY SMALL: THE WORLD OF THE 17TH-CENTURY MICROSCOPISTS

*. . . Wherever I found out anything remarkable, I have thought it
my duty to put down my discovery on paper, so that all ingenious
people might be informed thereof.*

—Antony van Leeuwenhoek

The man who would close the final link in Harvey's argument about the
circulation of the blood was Marcello Malpighi. Born in 1628, the same
year that Harvey's great book was published, Malpighi was one of a new
breed of scientific investigators. The "microscopists" of the 17th century
were less concerned with the big ideas and big theories than were their
scientific cousins. For them the world was in the very small, in the "facts"
before their eyes. Theirs were for the most part voyages of discovery.
Unencumbered by the philosophical baggage of the past, they sought only
to record what their eyes could see and not to correct the old beliefs or to
create new ones.

No one knows exactly when the first true microscope was invented. The
use of lenses can be traced back to the Assyrians long before the time of the
Greeks. Seneca, a Roman author and philosopher, recorded his observations
that a globe of clear water held in the proper position would magnify writing.
Ptolemy wrote a treatise on optics. Ground lenses were found in the ruins
of Pompeii and Nineveh. The Arabs used lenses, and in the 13th century
the alchemist and writer Roger Bacon wrote about the optical properties of

Early microscopes such as this one, used by Robert Hooke, enabled scientists to enter the world of the very small for the first time.
(Courtesy of Bausch & Lomb)

refracted light and the magnifying qualities of various lenses. In 1558 the Swiss naturalist, Konrad Gesner, whom we will meet in the next chapter, used magnifying lenses to study snail shells.

As close as can be ascertained, the Dutch microscope maker Zacharias Janssen was probably the first to use combined lenses to aid their magnifying power. The first of these compound microscopes was probably produced around 1590. By the middle of the 17th century, these and various other microscopes were in the hands of a small and dedicated group of men who were beginning to see what no human had ever observed before. Like the telescope discoveries of Galileo, their work too would add a new and major window into the world of nature and its mysteries. With the aid of the microscope, wrote Pierre Boral, the court physician to Louis XIV: "Minute insects are changed into a colossal monster . . . countless parts are discovered . . . new physics are opened."

MALPIGHI AND THE CAPILLARY

One of the first of the great microscopists, Marcello Malpighi (1628–94), was educated at the University of Bologna, where he obtained his medical degree in 1656. The atmosphere at Bologna was stifling and conservative. Candidates for medical degrees, for instance, were required to swear upon penalty of losing their degree that they would not treat any patients for more than three days who had not confessed and announced themselves to be devoted Catholics. And Malpighi [mahl-PEE-gee], always something of a rebel, left the University of Bologna soon after to become a professor at the University of Pisa. There he made friends with the forward-thinking mathematician and anatomist Giovanni Borelli. It was a friendship that lasted for many years and inspired both men. Malpighi and Borelli performed dissections together, spent many long hours discussing the advanced ideas of Galileo and Descartes and continued exchanging informative letters throughout their lives. Borelli had also begun making some discoveries with the aid of his microscope, and it was probably at Pisa that Malpighi began his major microscopic studies. Personal problems, though, eventually compelled him to return to Bologna, where he spent most of the rest of his life teaching and pursuing his microscopic observations.

Even as a young student Malpighi had been strongly impressed with the work of William Harvey, and he was a devoted admirer of Harvey's careful work in solving the problems of blood circulation. There was one major flaw in Harvey's persuasive argument though: In order to "close the loop" in the circulatory flow of the blood within the body, some link had to be discovered between the arteries and veins. Most of Harvey's followers assumed that the link had to exist, but because it was too tiny to be seen, it was still unproven.

A series of experiments and microscopic observations Malphighi made between 1660 and 1661 provided the key. Studying first the lungs of dogs and then turning to dissections and microscopic observations of hundreds of frogs and bats, he demonstrated that blood flowed through a complex network of vessels over the lungs. It was a major step in the eventual understanding of respiration, since now it was quickly understood how air could diffuse from the lungs into the bloodstream and be carried throughout the body.

Then Malpighi made his most important discovery. Microscopic study of the wing membranes of bats revealed small vessels (later called capillaries), invisible to the naked eye, connecting the smallest visible arteries to the smallest visible veins. The find at last provided the link to complete Harvey's circulatory system. More microscopic observations of still more frogs (he commented in a letter to Borelli that he felt as if he had "destroyed almost the whole race of frogs") verified his discoveries. He even hit upon the ingenious idea of injecting water into the pulmonary artery and watching it come out of the pulmonary vein. In effect, this washed the blood out of the lung, making lung tissue more transparent, and making the capillaries more visible. Harvey was right.

GIOVANNI BORELLI AND THE MECHANICAL BODY

The French philosopher and mathematician René Descartes exerted a tremendous influence on the thinkers of the 17th and 18th centuries. Although he was not a scientist and did no experimentation or original research, Descartes's theories about the mechanistic nature of the universe rivaled Newton's in their impact. Descartes argued that all the objects in the universe, not just stars and planets, but animals and humans, could be understood in purely mechanistic terms.

Giovanni Borelli (1608–79), an Italian mathematician and physiologist, was a close friend of the physiologist and microscopist Marcello Malpighi. There is no evidence that Borelli ever studied medicine officially; his early interests were mathematics and the new astronomy of Galileo, whom he greatly admired. Occupying a chair in mathematics at Pisa in 1656, he grew friendly with Malpighi and worked with him, performing a number of anatomical studies. Under the influence of Galileo and Descartes, Borelli developed the ambition to apply the mechanistic principles of the new way of thinking about the physical world to the working of the human body. In his book *De motu animalium* ("Concerning Animal Motion") he discussed the movements of individual muscles and groups of muscles using geometric and mechanical principles, such as those of the lever. He also studied posture in humans and animals and the mechanics of the flight of birds. He was less successful in trying to apply mechanical principles to the internal organs of the body. He believed that the stomach, for instance, was a simple grinding device and failed to recognize the digestive system as a chemical rather than a mechanical process.

Borelli's attempts to explain the working of the human body on strict mechanistic terms was not an isolated phenomenon in the late 17th century, though. Impressed by the many successes in physics of the Newtonian and Cartesian approaches, others also were attempting to answer the questions of living organisms using the new methods. In fact, two separate groups of investigators had begun to emerge by the beginning of the 18th century: the iatromechanists, who believed that all the functions of the living body could be explained with physical and mathematical principles based on the concepts of force and motion, and the iatrochemists, who believed that all the body functions could be explained as chemical events. Unfortunately for the development of a fuller understanding of physiology, the two opposing camps remained at odds for many years, each insisting that its own approach was the only valid one.

But Malpighi's work was not confined to his major discovery of the capillaries. He also turned his microscope to the study of plant anatomy and the developmental anatomy of plants and animals. Although, like most of his work, these investigations added immeasurably to scientific knowledge, his work investigating chick embryology had some misleading consequences. While the work was fine in many details, some of Malpighi's observations led him to believe mistakenly that he had found the developing form of a chick inside an egg that had not been incubated by a hen. This led many to the conclusion that he had discovered proof for an old idea that the new organism was already present, or preformed, in complete but miniature detail within the egg or sperm. Already some books of the time were showing pictures of completely formed tiny humans within sperm cells. Thus, this ancient philosophical idea was for a while given some apparent scientific validity it didn't deserve.

GREW FOCUSES ON THE STRUCTURE OF PLANTS

Not all of the microscopists concentrated so heavily on animal physiology. One of the most active of the 17th-century microscopists, the English physician Nehemiah Grew (1641–1712), turned his microscope primarily on plants. His studies into what might be called plant anatomy led him to recognize the flowers as the sexual organs of plants. He discovered the pistils (feminine) and the stamen (masculine) and recognized their place in the reproductive process. He also discovered the pollen grains produced by the stamen, the equivalent of the sperm cells in the animal world.

SWAMMERDAM AND THE INSECT WORLD

The young Dutch naturalist, Jan Swammerdam (1637–80), turned his microscopes primarily toward the insect kingdom. In his tragically short, agonized life (he was subject to intense periods of mental instability, depression and melancholia), Swammerdam [SVAHM-er-dahm] turned his lens on more than 3,000 species of insects. Compulsively and almost obsessively methodical, he also performed autopsies on animals and humans and became an expert on comparative anatomy. He obtained his medical degree in 1667 but never established a regular practice. Although he is most famous for his discovery of the red blood corpuscles (later to be recognized as the oxygen-carrying structure of the blood), the bulk of Swammerdam's work was on insects, earning him the title of the world's first true entomologist.

Working with his thousands of tiny insects, Swammerdam pioneered many new dissecting techniques and developed dozens of new miniaturized instruments for his work. Examining one of his favorite subjects, the honeybee, he was the first to discover that the "king" was actually a female, that the drones were males and that the rest, or ordinary bees, were neuter females, which he named workers.

Swammerdam's scientific work ended when he joined an extremely fanatic and obscure religious cult in 1673, but his private zoological museum (which he had unsuccessfully tried to sell along with his instruments and books) contained more than 3,000 insects all carefully dissected and displayed. Broken by illness, overwork and his emotional involvement in the activities of the cult, he died in 1680 at the young age of 43. Although his writings were largely unpublished during his life, two volumes of his collected work on insect anatomy published posthumously in 1737–38, entitled *Biblia naturae* ("Bible of Nature"), became recognized, nearly 100 years after his birth, as the best study of insect microanatomy of the 18th century.

HOOKE, MASTER ILLUSTRATOR

Second only to Swammerdam in his microscopic studies of insects was the versatile and controversial physicist, Robert Hooke. Known primarily for his studies of light and his famous quarrels with Isaac Newton (see Part One), Hooke was also an accomplished microscopist. His book *Micrographia* ("Tiny drawings"), published in 1665, contained some of the most exacting and beautiful drawings ever made of microscopic studies. The series of 57 illustrations, most of them drawn by Hooke himself (although some may have been done by the brilliant architect Christopher Wren), showed such wonders as the eye of a fly, the shape of the stinging organ of a bee, flea and louse anatomies, the structure of feathers and the form of molds. The *Micrographia* also contained Hooke's theory of fossils, later proven to be correct but then a subject of high dispute, and detailed his theories of the physics of light and color along with his ideas on respiration and combustion. His most famous microscopic observations were his discovery and studies of the honeycomb structure of the cork plant, which he called "cells" because they resembled the monastic cells that monks lived in at the time. He observed a similar texture in a number of plants and, although he did not know for certain what the purpose of such cells could be, he thought that they might serve as channels to carry fluids through the plant material, in the same way that arteries and veins serve the same function in the animal body.

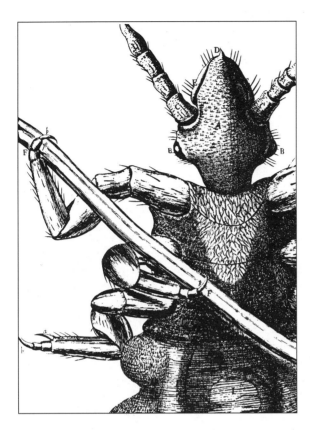

Drawing by Robert Hooke of a head louse and a human hair
(Robert Hooke: *Micrographia*, 1665)

LEEUWENHOEK'S SMALL WORLD

Without a doubt the most remarkable of the 17th-century microscopists was a self-educated Dutch microscope maker by the name of Antony van Leeuwenhoek [LAY-ven-hook]. Called by many the greatest amateur scientist and microscopist of the 17th century, Leeuwenhoek was born in Delft, Holland on October 24, 1632. His father was a basket maker and his mother the daughter of a town brewer. (The picturesque old town of Delft was known for its fine china and its beer.) Leeuwenhoek's childhood wasn't particularly remarkable. His father died when the boy was young, his mother remarried happily, and Leeuwenhoek received a normal upbringing for the time with a fairly standard grammar school education. At the age of 16 he was sent to Amsterdam to become apprentice to a draper in the dry-goods business. There he spent most of his time as a cashier. His apprenticeship completed, he returned to Delft in 1654 and opened up his own dry-goods business. He married at the age of 22 and had two children, and as his dry-goods business prospered he found himself appointed to a variety of

117

municipal positions in the small town. On the surface, he was a typical and fairly successful small-town businessman, little different from dozens of other middle-class shopkeepers in the quiet streets of Delft. He kept regular hours, sound habits and a respectable reputation. He dressed appropriately for his class and acted in keeping with custom and a clear conscience.

Someplace along the way, though, Leeuwenhoek began constructing microscopes. It may have started as a hobby, or as a part of his trade; it was the custom of the better drapers to use magnifying lenses to inspect the quality of their linen. When exactly he turned his lenses away from simply examining linen and toward other things is not known. Certainly though it was an activity that must have started early. The hundreds of superbly crafted microscopes that he developed were much more powerful and ingenious than were necessary for the simple needs of a draper. All of Leeuwenhoek's microscopes were single-lensed. The double-lensed, or compound, microscopes of the time were powerful but were notoriously troubled with chromatic aberration: everything observed in them appeared to be surrounded by fringes of color. That meant that trying to study very small details was difficult at best and sometimes impossible. The trick was

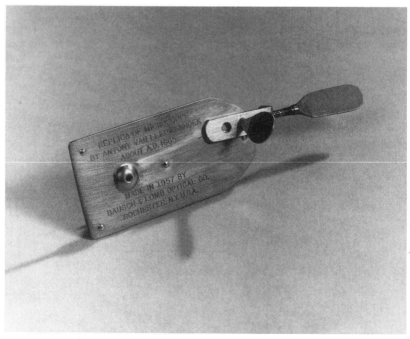

A replica of one of Leeuwenhoek's microscopes (Courtesy of Bausch & Lomb)

to build a single-lensed microscope with the power of a compound lens, but without its aberration problems. The solution that Leeuwenhoek came up with was a single lens, carefully ground in the form of a small glass bead and set in a hole drilled into a brass plate. The object to be studied was then held in place and its distance from the lens was adjusted either forward or backward by different kinds of moving pin arrangements. The microscope was used most of the time by simply holding the whole thing up to the light and looking through it. The tiny and nearly spherical form of Leeuwenhoek's lens allowed for great power—one, still in existence, magnifies objects about 275 times their normal size—but it also demanded intense concentration and often caused severe eye strain.

The first recognition of Leeuwenhoek's unique talent in building and using his microscopes came in 1673 when the physician and anatomist Regnier de Graaf wrote a letter to the British Royal Society in London. Although he was already suffering from an illness that would cut his life tragically short, de Graaf had a secure reputation for his own scientific work. His letter, announcing that the unknown draper named Antony van Leeuwenhoek built the best microscopes that he had ever seen, caught the attention of the society president. Along with his letter de Graaf also forwarded a letter that Leeuwenhoek had sent to him describing some of his activities and observations. The letter contained Leeuwenhoek's microscopic observations on mold, the mouths of bees and the common louse. It was enough to perk up the president's interest, and he wrote to Leeuwenhoek asking for more details and sketches. Leeuwenhoek wrote back that he could supply the details but that since he couldn't draw he would have to have the drawings done for him.

What may have started condescendingly at first, for Leeuwenhoek wrote in simple colloquial Dutch and demonstrated little understanding of scientific protocol, soon began a parade of letters between the amateur scientist and the Royal Society. The letters, a remarkable 372 in all, continued throughout Leeuwenhoek's long life (he died in 1723 at the age of 91) and established a 50-year correspondence that was one of the most unusual in scientific history.

Written in a plain and homespun style, the letters often began with some simple talk about life in Delft, or his personal habits, his pet dog, or his business upturns and downturns, and then moved on to describing his amazing variety of microscopic observations. Often three or four different and unrelated sets of observations were included in each letter—not the usual way of doing things—and the secretary of the society patiently organized more traditional extracts for the society members. If the personal aspects of his communications were casual and homey, the reports of his hundreds of observations were made with painstaking care and exactness.

Antony van Leeuwenhoek usually held his microscope up to the light to make his observations. (Parke-Davis, Division of Warner-Lambert Company)

And what they reported quickly made him the most famous and respected microscopist in the world.

More than any other single individual in the 17th century, Leeuwenhoek opened up the world of the very small. Just as Galileo in the earlier part of the century had used his telescope to expand human awareness of the heavens and the cosmic world, so Leeuwenhoek, turning his microscope to such everyday things as the scrapings from his own teeth and drops of water, revealed another undreamed of dimension. Like Galileo he saw what no human had ever seen before, and by doing so he altered forever humanity's understanding of nature.

Although he made many discoveries in his journeys into the microscopic world, including his confirmation of Malpighi's discovery of the capillaries and his discovery of spermatozoa in seminal fluid, it was Leeuwenhoek's discovery of "living animalcules" that most astounded his contemporaries. Studying a drop of water under his lens, he found an amazing surprise: little "wretched beasties." "They stop, they stand still as 'twere upon a point," he wrote, "and then turn themselves round with that swiftness as we see a top turn round, the circumference they make being no bigger than that of a fine grain of sand." Even more amazing, in a letter dated October 9, 1676, he wrote that other *little animals, which drifted among the three sorts aforesaid, were incredibly small; nay, so small, in my sight, that I judged that even if 100 of these very wee animals lay stretched out one against another, they could not reach to the length of a grain of coarse sand; and if this be true, then ten hundred thousand of these living creatures could scarce equal the bulk of a coarse sand-grain. I discovered yet a fifth sort, which had about the thickness of the last-said animalcules, but were nearly twice as long.*

And in still another letter, dated 1683, he wrote

'Tis my wont of a morning to rub my teeth with salt, and then swill my mouth out with water: and, often, after eating, to clean my back teeth with a toothpick, as well as rubbing them hard with a cloth. . . .Yet notwithstanding, my teeth are not so cleaned thereby, but what there sticketh or groweth between some of my front ones and my grinders . . . a little white matter, which is as thick as if 'twere batter. . . . I almost always saw, with great wonder, that in the said matter there were many very little living animalcules, very prettily a-moving.

The world it seemed was teeming with much more life than had ever before been imagined! Living creatures existed in drops of water, and the tiny particles lodged between a person's teeth!

Leeuwenhoek had observed a fantastic new micro-universe of protozoa and bacteria. And, although much of what he discovered would not be completely understood until many years later, the painstaking methods and insatiable curiosity of this unassuming Dutch draper would lay the foundations for others to follow and would bring him more fame in his lifetime than he ever dreamed.

In 1680 Leeuwenhoek was elected a member of the Royal Society, the most prestigious scientific society in the world at the time. It was a heady leap for a self-educated shopkeeper. And although he was almost overwhelmed at the honor, he wasn't too happy with the steady stream of visitors it brought to his quiet home in Delft. At one point he noted that he had received 26 people in four days. One day he was even visited by Peter the Great of Russia, who sailed up the canal on a special "canal yacht." Leeuwenhoek dutifully lugged some of his instruments and specimens down to the boat, since the royal visitor didn't want to attract admiring crowds in the city.

But the attention did not slow his work. In 1716, when Leeuwenhoek was 84 years old, the University of Louvain awarded him a medal and a eulogistic poem written in Latin, the equivalent today of an honorary degree. Because he did not read Latin, the poem was read to him, bringing "tears to my eyes" as he wrote later to the Royal Society.

He remained active up to the time of his death in 1723, and his final letter to the society, mailed by his daughter, bequeathed to them a cabinet containing 26 of his very finest and most beloved silver microscopes.

Together Malpighi, Grew, Swammerdam, Hooke and the estimable Leeuwenhoek brought not only an added dimension to the investigations into the life sciences, but a new and unbiased approach to those investigations. While none could be said to be without a philosophy, for the most part each peered into his microscope to discover and record what he saw there rather than to prove or disprove some ancient or new theory. With few exceptions, most of the 17th-century microscopists, the acknowledged "Big Five" and many others of lesser fame, sought not to create ideas for others to follow but to follow instead the facts that might be discovered in the lenses of their instruments. They were not big thinkers, but each added to the store of knowledge that others with greater or more profound visions would use to build and test theories. Thanks to the microscopists, a new and useful tool had been given to science, one that even today, in both its most simple and basic form and its most sophisticated high-tech designs, continues to gather facts and to open up new and exciting views of nature.

C H A P T E R   1 0

UNDERSTANDING THE DIVERSITY OF LIFE

*T*oday newspaper, magazine and television commentators tell us that we are experiencing an information explosion. Thanks to the efficiency and speed of modern technologies such as computers, television satellites and new printing methods, new discoveries, ideas, facts and theories pour into our homes each day. It's a tough job to keep track of it all and even tougher to understand what it all means. During the 17th century humanity was experiencing a similar momentous burst of new information. The great wave of exploration after Columbus brought Europeans new knowledge of a multitude of exotic lands, animals, plants and peoples. The Renaissance opened up new possibilities of intellectual and artistic expression. The scientific revolution shattered long-held traditional views of nature and humans, replacing them with new and testable facts and theories.

It was a heady time for everyone, including those in the fields of botany and zoology who were concerned with keeping track of and describing all the new discoveries in the plant and animal kingdoms.

Collecting and describing nature's wonders was a tradition that stretched back to the ancient Greeks. Such collections, called herbals and bestiaries by the scholars of the medieval ages, were intended not only to inform the learned of the wide diversity of God's creations but to instruct the reader about their usable properties, their wonders or their edifying capabilities.

For the 17th century, though, simply throwing together descriptions and pictures of plants or animals was not enough. That would be something like taking a couple of hundred baseball cards and tossing them willy-nilly into a large basket. Some method was needed to organize all the collected knowledge, to find some useful systems to classify the items in the collection.

From an herbal by Duret (published in 1605), illustrating the belief that fish develop from fruit that drops from the tree into the water and birds from fruit that falls on the land (Library of the U.S. Department of Agriculture)

With the baseball cards you might try to arrange groupings of all the players who played on the same teams, all the New York Yankees past and present in one place, all the Chicago Cubs in another. Or you might group together players by position, all the pitchers in one place, all the first basemen in another, or by the years each played, or by the batting averages, or the earned run averages. Or, of course, you could combine arrangements, making still finer groupings—say a group of all the New York Yankee hitters who batted over 300 between the years 1940 and 1960.

Organizing the amazing variety of plants and animals isn't that easy, though. Imagine now that you were creating a set of "nature cards" from scratch. You take your pencil and a pad of paper out to the woods somewhere and start drawing pictures of the various plants and animals that you see and write down descriptions of those plants and animals to go with the pictures you have drawn. At the end of a couple of months of work and several hundred pads of paper, you have a large basket filled with your collected information. You need to give it some kind of order. How do you start? It's probably going to be easy enough to separate the plants from the animals (although some tall tales got the Greeks and medieval scholars in trouble there), but how else do you begin to sort and catalog your collection? Usually you will look for certain similarities, things held in common. You might start by grouping together certain plants that look alike, ones that you can eat and ones that you can not eat, or separating large animals from small, land creatures from water creatures, creatures that fly from creatures that do not. There are obviously many ways that you could make your groupings, some more effective than others.

Because he was a philosopher in the time of a great burst of learning, Aristotle gave himself even a bigger chore. He decided to try to gather up a collection of information about all living things—not just plants and animals but humans, earthworms and all other creatures, and then arrange this information into a system of various groupings.

These groupings formed the beginnings of an idea that would later be called the "Great Chain of Being." Actually, in Aristotle's thought, it was more a "ladder" of nature. He believed that everything on Earth could be arranged on a sort of a scale with inanimate matter on the bottom followed by plants, crustaceans, egg-bearing creatures (reptiles, birds, fishes, amphibians), mammals and, finally, humans at the top of the order. He also attempted, not always with success, to break down each of these "rungs" on his ladder into still other categories. He divided the animal kingdom, for instance, into groups possessing red blood and those without it (now called vertebrates and invertebrates). He also developed a theory of three "souls," which would also dominate much thinking into the Middle Ages. Only living things had souls, he taught. For plants, since they grew and reproduced, he postulated a "vegetative soul," while for animals that could move and feel in addition, he added an "animal soul," and for humans who could also think, he added a "rational soul." These souls were seen by Aristotle to be some kind of mysterious animating principle, which distinguished the animate from the inanimate objects.

Following Aristotle, although somewhat less ambitiously, the Greek botanist Theophrastus [thee-oh-FRAS-tus] (c. 372–287 B.C.), who had inherited Aristotle's library and conducted the Lyceum after Aristotle's retirement, continued his study of plants and described more than 550 species.

More important though was the work of the Greek physician Dioscorides (who lived around A.D. 50). The sources of medieval botany, the herbals, can for the most part be traced all the way back to this Greek thinker. Although a number of different works are often credited to him, the one manuscript that we can be sure is really his is usually referred to by its Latin name *De materia medica*. A military physician who studied plants primarily for their medical uses, Dioscorides was a careful and accurate observer. Mentioning about 500 plants, Dioscorides gave each plant a description and place of origin, plus the method of preparing the plant into a drug and its medicinal uses. Although some earlier versions of the work were thought to have included some kind of slightly more exacting system of arrangement, the one transported down through the centuries after his death was simply arranged alphabetically according to the name of the plant. It was a simple arrangement that many of the later herbals and bestiaries would follow. Like Galen, Dioscorides wanted the industry of his work to inspire others to follow in his footsteps and not simply to copy him. But copy him many did. Like Galen, Dioscorides became for medieval scholars the final authority to be followed slavishly and with complete, unquestioned devotion. His books were the law, to be read, studied and taught. Unfortunately, some of the books thought to be his were not, while others, which may have been authentic, were poor copies to say the least. More than a thousand years of hand copying had done serious damage to Dioscorides's original work. Passed down from copyist to copyist, small errors crept in and were magnified into bigger ones. Sometimes, taking artistic license, the copyists

Plant and animal classification was blocked for a long time by myths like the lamb of Tartary, illustrated here, a lamb that people believed grew on a plant stalk. (Library of the U.S. Department of Agriculture)

deliberately and thoughtlessly made changes of their own—extra leaves might be added to a plant for better-looking aesthetic balance on a page, unattractive flowers might be made to look more attractive, spindly roots might be made stouter. Outright ridiculousness also appeared occasionally as the copyist out of boredom or "inspiration" added more elaborate symbolic embellishments. A plant called the narcissus was illustrated with tiny humans crawling from its leaves, geese could be seen growing out of trees, and lambs were shown growing on plants.

The Bestiary, as it passed through the centuries, also had more than its share of problems. The most popular version of this wondrous collection of animals is thought to have originated in Alexandria some time around 200 A.D. And, although many copies and imitations were made throughout the years, the original itself was a compilation of many other works. It borrowed heavily from oral tales from Hellenic, Egyptian and Asiatic traditions, as well as the works of Aristotle and the famous Roman scholar, Pliny the Elder (A.D. 23–79). Pliny, who died observing the eruption of Vesuvius that destroyed the city of Pompeii, was an enyclopedic compiler whose major work, *Natural History*, attempted to summarize all the knowledge of the world in 37 volumes. Basically a digest borrowing from more than 2,000 ancient books and nearly 500 writers, it was a mixture of good, sound fact, common sense and incredibly bizarre and gullible fantasy. Not the most critical of thinkers, Pliny seems to have swallowed whole just about everything he read or heard. Such fabulous creatures could be found in the *Natural History* as men with the heads of dogs, turtles with gigantic shells that could be used for the roofs of houses, unicorns, mermaids, flying horses and many other wild and zany creations, all presented as fact with a straight face. Along with the nonsense he also included a strong array of factual information on less fantastic animals, astronomy, ecology, cooking, Greek painting, mining and just about anything else that interested him.

By the Middle Ages, the Bestiary and its many copies and derivatives had become popular reading as elaborately illustrated picture books of fabulous creatures. Their influence extended through the Renaissance and even up to the later part of the 17th century. Part of the reason for this was that in many ways such books became perfect vehicles for Christian moral instruction. Their fabulous creatures could be made to fit just about any purpose. The mythical phoenix for example "sets fire to itself of its own accord until it burns itself up. Then, verily, on the ninth day afterward, it rises from its own ashes! Now our Lord Jesus Christ exhibits the character of this bird. . . ." The ant-lion, a cross between a lion and an ant, was destined to starve because its ant nature would not eat meat while its lion nature would not permit it to eat plants—in the same way, according to the Bestiary, that all were destined to fail who tried to serve at once both God and the devil. Sometimes the moral stretched to two or three times the length of the description of the animal. Following this lead, many other "natural histories," such as *Causes and Cures* by St. Hildegard the Nun (1098–1179), became instruments to teach morals. In her book St. Hildegard used the Book of Genesis for her guide in organizing the plants and animals.

Because they carried such a heavy burden of fantasy, mythology and moralizing, it is not surprising that each new edition or copy of these bestiaries became further and further divorced from reality. As a result, they lost much of the effectiveness they might have had for the scientific understanding of natural history.

There were some exceptions. In the mid-13th century the brilliant and highly individualistic German emperor, Frederick II (1194–1250), published an excellent book on falconry titled *The Art of Hunting with Birds*. Forsaking the usual hodgepodge of fact and fiction, Frederick, who had little patience with superstition or scholastic pedantry, confined himself to his own acute observations. The result was a splendidly disciplined and accurate study of hundreds of different kinds of birds, complete with exact illustrations and faithful descriptions of their behavior, anatomy and physiology.

Frederick II was far ahead of his time, and his approach to first-hand and careful observation was not soon followed up. The scholastic Albertus Magnus (1183–c. 1280) published his *De animalibus* ("About Animals") around 1250, but it was little more than an ambitious rehash, occasionally skeptical, but for the most part still including the mythical animals and folklore of Aristotle, Pliny and others.

Some progress in descriptive botany was made during the Renaissance, most notably in the work of Otto Brunfels (1489–1534), Jerome Boch (1498–1554) and Leonhard Fuchs (1501–66), who are collectively sometimes called the "German Fathers of Botany." Each contributed collections that not only were better and more authentically illustrated than existing herbals but added many new and local plants. More important, their work, becoming popular, helped to establish the growing back-to-nature movement that was beginning to take a new, first-hand look at plants and animals. All three, though, were still under the influence of Dioscorides. Fuchs, whose *Natural History* is the best known, based his text more or less directly on Dioscorides and arranged his plants alphabetically, although he did try his hand at establishing a basic botanical terminology.

KONRAD GESNER, NATURAL HISTORIAN

The most influential of the new "natural histories" was Konrad Gesner's *Historia Animalium* ("History of Animals") begun in 1551. Gesner (1516–65) was a Swiss naturalist with an encyclopedic range of interests and an amazing

FOSSILS

Fossils (petrified objects with the appearance of plants, animal bones, shells and teeth) had been known and discussed since Aristotle. During the Renaissance such scholars as Konrad Gesner collected and displayed them in museums and cabinets. A great argument began to rage during the 16th and 17th centuries as to their exact nature and origin. Some naturalists, such as Bernard Pallisy (1510–90), Nicolaus Steno (1638–86) and Robert Hooke (1635–1703) argued that they were petrified animal and plant remains that had been infiltrated into solid rock by floods, perhaps even the biblical flood of Noah. Others, though, were disturbed by the existence of so many fossils of species no longer seen. They seemed to call into question the religious belief held by Christians that God the Creator was perfect and would not allow a species to perish. This group came to a variety of conclusions. Some believed that fossils were direct productions of nature in their own right that formed like crystals. Others thought that they were Plato's ideal forms, which were free-floating and simply embedded themselves into rocks. And still others, though few serious thinkers, argued that they were tests of God, placed in rocks to test the faith of humankind with their riddle.

By the late 17th century, though, the recognition that fossils were organic remains began to win the day. Advances in the study of geology during the 18th century would finally convince most reasonable thinkers of the validity of this argument.

---

store of energy. His *Historia Animalium* was a gigantic encyclopedia of five volumes, comprising more than 4,000 pages. A prolific encyclopedist, he also wrote a "Universal Library," an elaborate bibliography listing all the the known books in Greek, Hebrew and Latin, complete with summaries of their contents. Too busy to do much observing of animals himself, he used the work of a wide variety of correspondents to put *Historia Animalium* together. Gesner made no attempt at classification and he, like others, employed a simple alphabetical arrangement "in order to facilitate the use of the work." Like the older bestiaries, Gesner's work included its share of bizarre creatures, including a bird of paradise who laid her eggs in a hollow on the back of the male because she flew so high she had no nesting sites and the basilisk, a lizard monster hatched by a serpent from the egg of a rooster. To his credit, Gesner distinguished in his commentary between these fanciful creatures and more realistic ones, including both the believable and the unbelievable for the sake of completeness. For each animal Gesner described the habits and behavior, its means of capture and its uses

In his Historia Animalium, *Gesner included both fanciful creatures and accurately drawn representations based on careful observation.* (Konrad Gesner: *Historia Animalium liber*, 1551–58)

as food or medicine. Gesner's work was extremely popular, pretty much superseding all the previous works for serious students of natural history for more than 100 years.

By the late 17th century, though, people again began to wonder if there were not some way to organize all the new information pouring in about plants and animals. The situation, thanks to so many new discoveries from around the world, was chaotic. Aristotle had described around 500 species of animals. At the beginning of the 17th century only around 6,000 species of plants were known. By the end of the century the number of known plants had jumped to nearly 12,000. People studying animals had a similar problem. Today we know that there are between 1,000,000 to 20,000,000 (estimates vary) species of living things on Earth. There was simply too much new information coming in too fast for anyone to be able to study and understand it all. Alphabetical catalogs were not the answer. For one thing, just where a particular plant or animal might be found in each book depended upon the language the book was written in. Naturalists needed some better way of naming plants and animals that broke across the language barrier. They also needed a clearer understanding of what they meant when they spoke of a particular "kind" of plant or animal. Were there basic categories or units in nature? The startling discoveries in the world of 17th-century physics had demonstrated that there appeared to be natural laws acting to create order in the physical universe. Shouldn't there then be some similar laws or rules that, once discovered, could help create order in the increasingly complex world of plants and animals?

Although the solution to this problem would have to wait many years, a major step toward it was taken in the late 17th century by the work of the English naturalist, John Ray.

JOHN RAY AND THE SPECIES CONCEPT

Born in Black Notley, Essex, England on November 29, 1628, Ray was the son of a village blacksmith. Devoutly religious, he was educated at Cambridge and received his Master's degree in 1651. He was from the beginning a keen observer of plants and animals as well as a strong believer in the ancient Aristotelian scale of nature in which each and every living being had its unchanging place in a rigid hierarchy that stretched from the lowest forms to the highest. His observations made throughout England and Europe convinced him though that both plants and animals could be roughly systematized and grouped into basic units that would allow a clearer understanding of their nature and relationships.

FRANCESCO REDI AND SPONTANEOUS GENERATION

Well into the 17th century many people believed that flies and other insects arose spontaneously from urine, garbage or other decaying matter. Some believed that animals as large as rats arose spontaneously in heaps of garbage, and that frogs, crabs and salamanders arose directly from slime. The physician and alchemist Jan Baptista van Helmont even offered a recipe for home-grown mice that used the ingredients of bran and old rags stuffed in a bottle and left in a dark closet. The first to look at the question scientifically was an Italian physician named Francesco Redi.

One of the least-known of the 17th-century experimenters, Redi (1626–98) could have walked right out of the Renaissance. A literary scholar, linguist, poet and scientist, he cut a dashing figure in Pisa and became the personal physician of two grand dukes of Tuscany, Ferdinand II and Cosimo III. Redi's most famous work in science was his series of simple and carefully planned experiments that helped to shed further doubt on the popular idea of spontaneous generation.

In one experiment, typical of the many experiments that he ran, Redi sealed a dead snake, some fish and pieces of veal in large jars, placing similar samples in open jars as controls. The sealed matter did not produce maggots, while the matter in the open jars did. He repeated the experiments, covering half of his jars with gauze tops instead of sealing them, thus letting the air in but keeping flies out. No maggots appeared in the gauze-covered jars, either.

"Thus the flesh of dead animals cannot engender worms unless the eggs of the living be deposited therein," Redi wrote. It did not completely disprove the idea of spontaneous generation; those who wanted to believe in it still did, but it was a strong blow.

A member of the Italian Accademia del Cimento (Academy of Experiments), Redi was also a vocal proponent for the new scientific method, advocating that "all their efforts be concentrated upon experimentation, upon the creation of standards of measurement and exact methods of research."

Ray's basic insight was to define the concept of "species." A species is a population of organisms in which the members are able to breed among themselves and produce fertile offspring. Writing in 1686, he explained:

After a long and considerable investigation, no surer criteria for determining species has occurred to me than the distinguishing features that perpetuate themselves in propagation from seed. Thus, no matter what variations occur in the individual or the species, if they spring from the seed of the one and the same plant, they are accidental variations and not such as to distinguish a species.

The same rule applied to animals. A bull and a cow were to be seen as members of the same species because when they mate they produce off-spring like themselves. Trivial variations such as the colors of a plant's flowers, or the size of an animal's offspring, or an animal's habits, could no longer be seen as the basis of a species. Ray also dealt a major blow to the monsters and bizarre creatures that had inhabited bestiaries for centuries with his assertion that "forms which are different in species always retain their specific natures, and one species does not grow from the seed of another species." And although he retained his Aristotelian belief in the rigid fixity of species, he also recognized that some variation through mutation could be possible. It was not the complete answer to the problems of classification, but it was a major first step toward unscrambling a very jumbled picture.

A prolific writer, Ray's most important books were *Historia plantarum generalis* ("A General Account of Plants"), a three-volume set written between 1686 and 1704, and *Synopsis methodica animalium quadrupedum* ("Synopsis of Four-Footed Beasts"), published in 1693. In these works and others he attempted to establish some new systematic ways of looking at plants and animals based on their anatomical similarities—for instance distinguishing between animals with a two- versus a four-chambered heart, and classifying "hairy quadrupeds" into "hooved" and "clawed" groups.

Ray never really succeeded in setting up a complete and acceptable system of classification for plants and animals before dying in Black Notley on January 17, 1705. Although his concept of species gave a good handle for those who came after him, many of his other ideas were superseded by the work of the brilliant 18th-century Swedish botanist, Carolus Linnaeus (1707–78). Born two years after Ray's death, Linnaeus would go on to develop the first modern system of classification and become the founder of modern taxonomy. More important, Linnaeus's work would open up the way for others to begin new and deeper investigations into the kingdoms of life on Earth and the origin and relationships of all living things.

E P I L O G U E

The world had changed dramatically by the end of the 17th century. The Renaissance and the scientific revolution had chartered new territories in humanity's understanding of itself and the world of nature. Humanity's geographical and intellectual horizons had broadened to stretch from the narrow confines of ancient times and the Middle Ages to reach the threshold of the Enlightenment and the Industrial Revolution— the great movements of the 18th century that would open the doors to the modern world.

"If I have seen further it is by standing on the shoulders of giants," Isaac Newton had said. From the time of the ancient Greeks to the end of the 17th century the world had known such giants: Aristotle, Plato, Copernicus, Leonardo, Kepler, Tycho, Galileo, Vesalius, Harvey, a dozen others and Newton himself. They had given the world new ways to understand nature and freed it from many of the old ways of thinking. Entering the 18th century, humanity looked at nature with different eyes and a new understanding. No longer would the statement of facts be left to unsupported authority. Observation would guide the mind. Nature would no longer be thought of as manipulated by the capriciousness of the gods, but could be understood as a self-acting, self-perpetuating system. Changes in nature could be seen to follow natural and understandable laws. Most disturbing for many, perhaps, the Earth was no longer the center of the universe, and soon would follow the realization that humanity was not the purpose of the universe's existence.

Indeed, for most scientists, by the end of the 17th century, purpose in nature was no longer a scientifically valid concept.

The temper of the times for science was the belief that the universe and everything in it could be viewed and understood as a vast machine and the job of science was to use the new scientific methods to uncover the mechanisms that made the machine work. It was an idea that swept the intellectual communities of the western world. Not everyone was happy with it, though, and it wasn't always helpful. In many areas of biology, for instance, the mechanistic way of thinking was often a hindrance. For a long time the strict mechanists in biology thought that the warmth of blood was caused by the

135

friction of the blood moving within the blood vessels. But this mechanistic view did break away from the sterile attitudes of the scholastics and the traditional views of mystical causes and explanations for the workings of the world—and it established the enduring power of the scientific method to solve many of the problems and mysteries of nature. By the 18th century many people outside science, such as social thinkers, politicians and philosophers, were also attempting to introduce the new scientific methods to their disciplines. These, too, while often dramatic, were not always successful. Eventually a reaction was bound to set in, and it did, in the late 18th century—with a return by many to traditional religion, new forms of ancient occult beliefs and a new movement called romanticism, the beginning of a new social split between science and society that in many ways has lasted up to this day.

Science, though, and the power of the scientific method (or *methods*, since few scientists today would claim allegiance to only one method) have triumphantly endured. Indeed, to many, science remains the most beautiful and profound of all human endeavors.

Today scientists continue to probe the mysteries of nature. And the mysteries of nature continue to unfold like Chinese boxes. Such is the nature of nature and such is the nature of humanity.

"I do not know what I may appear to the world, but to myself I seem to have been only like a boy playing on the seashore, and diverting myself in now and then finding another smoother pebble, or a prettier shell than ordinary, while the great ocean of truth lay all undiscovered before me," wrote Newton.

And as the novelist, essayist and poet Robert Louis Stevenson wrote in a poem for children, "The world is so full of a number of things, I'm sure we should all be as happy as kings." In such a spirit does science thrive, and in such a spirit, long will it endure.

C H R O N O L O G Y

THE ANCIENTS TO THE HIGH MIDDLE AGES
2000 B.C.–A.D. 1428

2000 B.C.	The Babylonians develop a calendar system, observe the Sun, Moon and planets
1300 B.C.	The Phoenicians develop alphabets
1216 B.C.	Earliest known weather records in China
1100 B.C.	The Dorians complete their takeover of the Mycenaeans, occupying the area now known as Greece
763 B.C.	Babylonians make the first recorded observation of an eclipse of the Sun
753 B.C.	Rome is founded, according to tradition
750–701 B.C.	Homer and Hesiod, first known poets of the Greek culture, write their works
720 B.C.	First Chinese record of a solar eclipse
c. 624–c. 546 B.C.	Thales of Miletus (in what is now known as Turkey) proposes that water is the basis of all things
c. 610–c. 545 B.C.	Anaximander of Miletus, astronomer and philosopher, makes the first known attempt to write a history of the universe, developing a model of the Earth based on scientific principles
c. 570–500 B.C.	Anaximenes of Miletus, possibly a pupil of Anaximander, proposes that air is the fundamental substance of which all things in the universe are composed
c. 560–c. 480 B.C.	Pythagoras and his followers develop arithmetic and geometry. During this same period, the Chinese introduce advances in mathematics and the Indians develop a geometry
c. 540–c. 475 B.C.	Heraclitus of Ephesus (Turkey), Greek philosopher, teaches that change is the essence of all being, proposes fire as the primary substance
538 B.C.	The Persians conquer Babylon

530 B.C.–?	Alcmaeon, Greek Pythagorean physician, first person known to have dissected human cadavers for scientific purposes
c. 500 B.C.	Hindu thinkers recognize atomism as the basis of matter; steel is made in India
c. 500–c. 428 B.C.	Anaxagorus introduces the scientific spirit into Athens during the days of Pericles; authors a scientific treatise, *On Nature*
c. 490 B.C.	Leucippus, Greek philosopher, introduces the first idea of the atom in Western thought
483 B.C.	Religious reformer Buddha (Gautama Siddhartha) dies
479–80 B.C.	The Greeks stop the western expansion of Persia
c. 470–399 B.C.	Socrates, Greek philosopher whose chief disciple is Plato
c. 470–c. 371 B.C.	Democritus, Greek philosopher, expands on the teachings of Leucippus about atoms as indivisible bodies
461 B.C.	The Age of Pericles begins in Greece, a period when peace and good economic times allow culture and philosophy to develop
c. 427–c. 347 B.C.	Plato, Greek philosopher and teacher, whose Academy and teachings had enormous influence—especially his concepts of idealism and mathematical perfection—not only in his time, but for centuries afterward, especially during the Renaissance, and still today
384–322 B.C.	Aristotle, Greek philosopher and teacher, Plato's greatest student, attempts the first unified theory of the cosmos, as well as contributing to concepts in every field from physics to the life sciences
356–323 B.C.	Alexander the Great, who succeeds Philip II in 336, then begins a series of conquests that spread Greek culture as far east as India and as far south as Egypt
341–270 B.C.	Epicurus of Samos founds a philosophical school in which atoms are a basic part of the philosophy
338 B.C.	Philip II of Macedon overpowers the Greek forces and becomes head of all Greek states except Sparta
c. 325–c. 270 B.C.	Euclid, Greek mathematical philosopher, founds Euclidean geometry
c. 310–c. 230 B.C.	Aristarchus of Samos, Greek astronomer
300 B.C.	The Museum at Alexandria is built, which becomes a center for scholars and artists, especially Greek mathematicians
c. 287–212 B.C.	Archimedes, Greek mathematician and engineer

264 B.C.	First Punic War, between Rome and Carthage, begins
c. 262–c. 190 B.C.	Apollonius of Perga, Greek mathematician
c. 190–120 B.C.	Hipparchus of Nicea (Turkey), astronomer, composes a list of fixed stars
48 B.C.	The Library at Alexandria burns
44 B.C.	Julius Caesar, Roman leader, is assassinated
31 B.C.	Egypt (ruled by Cleopatra) falls to Rome
c. 20–?	Dioscorides, Greek physician and author of the first systematic pharmacopeia
A.D. 23–79	Pliny the Elder, Roman scholar, writer of *Naturalis historia* ("History of Nature")
c. 100	Chang Heng (Zhang Heng) introduces a grid system for mapmaking
c. 100–170	Ptolemy, Greek astronomer, whose system of the universe became the standard concept until the time of Copernicus 13 centuries later
c. 130–c. 200	Galen, Greek physician, whose extensive works became the primary resource on anatomy in the Middle Ages
541–544	The bubonic plague hits Europe and Asia Minor, killing as many as 10,000 people a day in Constantinople at its worst
616	The Visigoths invade Spain and take it from the Roman Empire
622	In a flight known as the Hegira, Mohammed flees Mecca for Medina. Islamic timekeeping begins with this year
632	Mohammed dies, Islamic expansion begins
711	Arab armies invade Spain
732	Charles Martel defeats the Islamic armies, ending the Islamic expansion
800	Charlemagne is crowned king of the Franks and Roman emperor of the West by the pope on Christmas Day, reviving the idea of a western Roman Empire for a time
1006	Chinese astronomers observe and record a nova
1054	Chinese astronomers observe and record a second nova in the night skies. Also observed in Japan and in the Arab countries
1066	William the Conqueror defeats Harold at the Battle of Hastings, establishing domination of England by Normandy (now in northern France)

c. 1100	Chinese geologist Chu Hsi (Zhu Xi) establishes that mountains are elevated land masses that once formed the sea floor
1126–1198	Averroës, Arab philosopher, known for his thoughtful and thorough commentaries on Aristotle
c. 1150	The Chinese develop the first rockets
1167 or 1168	Oxford University is founded in England
1215	English barons force King John to sign the Magna Carta
1222	The University of Padua (Italy) is founded. It is followed over the next 20 years by the founding of the University of Naples (Italy), the University of Toulouse (France), Cambridge University (England) and the University of Rome (Italy)
c. 1225–1274	Thomas Aquinas, Italian theologian who synthesized Catholic Christian doctrine and Aristotelian philosophy
1271	The main thrust of the Crusades, a series of attempts on the part of Christian armies to recapture the Holy Land (now Israel) from Islam, comes to an end
1271–1295	Marco Polo of Venice travels to the Far East
c. 1285–1349	William of Ockham, English thinker, introduces the idea that when several explanations of a phenomenon are offered, one must take the simplest—the concept known as Ockham's razor that has become one of the foundations of science
1346–47	Italian ships bring rats carrying bubonic plague to Europe, where 25 million—one-third of the population of the continent—die of the disease by 1351. Over the next 80 years, as the plague strikes again and again in waves, it kills three-fourths of the European population
1368	Establishment of the Ming dynasty in China, with the overthrow of the Mongols
1400	The Chinese pinpoint the length of the solar year at about 365.25 days
1415	European expansion begins with the Portuguese capture of Ceuta, on the African shore across from Gibraltar
1428	Joan of Arc leads French armies against the English

THE RENAISSANCE AND
THE SCIENTIFIC REVOLUTION
1449–1704

1449–92	The Renaissance reaches its height in Florence under the Medici family
1453	End of Byzantine Empire and the Hundred Years' War
1454	Gutenberg Bible published
1470	Mainspring for the clock invented
1473–1543	Nicolaus Copernicus, Polish astronomer
1492	Columbus lands in the Americas and the great age of exploration begins
1497	Portuguese explorer Vasco da Gama rounds the Cape of Good Hope
1502	Amerigo Vespucci explores the coast of South America
1504	Small mainspring put into a watch: first hand-held clocks
1509–64	John Calvin, French theologian, establishes a more radical form of Protestantism, which comes to be called Calvinism
1510–90	Ambroise Paré, French barber-surgeon, improved surgical methods
1514–64	Andreas Vesalius, Flemish anatomist
1517	Martin Luther nails 95 Theses on church door in Wittenberg, Saxony, marking the beginning of the Reformation
1523	Magellan circumnavigates the globe
1530	Gonzalo Jimenez de Quesada discovers the potato, which along with maize and tobacco becomes one of the most important botanical contributions made to Europe by the "New World" (important in trade)
1531	Francisco Pizarro lands in Peru (exterminates the Incas) and Spaniards claim most of Americas up to what is now the United States (except Brazil)
1533	King Henry VIII of England marries Anne Boleyn and begins movement toward establishment of Anglicanism
1530s	Six comets appear in sky; 1538, Girolamo Fracastoro publishes book recording observations of comets, including fact that tail always points away from the Sun

1539	Hernando DeSoto explores southeast portion of United States. Members of his party are the first Europeans to see the Mississippi River
1540	Peter Bennewitz, German, studying same comets publishes book in which he independently arrives at same conclusions and includes first scientific drawing of a comet.
1540	German mathematician Georg Joachim von Lauchen (1514–76), known as Rheticus, established improved trigonometry tables; his pamphlet published 1540 made first introduction of Copernicus's heliocentric ideas, preparing the way for Copernicus's theories and enabling computational astronomy to take a big leap forward
1540s	Interior of American continents explored—Hernando Cortés in New Mexico and Baja California
1543	Copernicus's *De revolutionibus* is published just before his death
1543	Vesalius's book, *De humanis corporis fabrica*, is published
1544–1603	William Gilbert, English investigator of magnetic and electrical phenomena
1546	The Wars of Religion begin when Holy Roman Emperor Charles V takes up arms against the Lutheran principalities
1546–1601	Tycho Brahe, Danish observational astronomer
1552	*Nostradamus*—gibberish verses predicting the future, which have been interpreted to have predicted the French Revolution, the rise of Napoleon, Hitler and World War II. But, since he included no dates, the validity of these predictions lies more in the hindsight of interpreters than the foresight of Nostradamus
1558	Elizabeth I becomes Queen of England
1559–61	Tobacco seeds exported for first time from America to France
1560	Italian physicist Giambattista della Porta (1535?–1615) founded first scientific association, the Academy of the Mysteries of Nature, later closed down by the Inquisition
1561–1626	Francis Bacon, founder of the scientific method
1568	Flemish geographer Gerhard Kremer (1512–94), known as Gerardus Mercator, perfected his cylindrical projection map

1572	Supernova is sighted in the constellation Cassiopeia; Tycho watched it for 485 days. First to scientifically observe a supernova, he tried to determine its parallax and could not detect it, so he figured it must be part of the heavens, beyond the Moon; he helped destroy the idea of the perfection and unchangingness of the heavens
1572	St. Bartholomew's Day (August 23); Catholics violate peace treaty by attacking and killing 50,000 unarmed Huguenots
1577	Tycho by now has set up the first completely outfitted astronomical observatory (though no telescope was yet invented) on the Island of Hven in the strait between Denmark and Sweden; he studies new comet appearing in the sky. Not able to find large parallax, he concludes this also is at a far distance beyond the Moon—yet another blow against Greek astronomical assumptions
1578	Sir Francis Drake, English navigator, sailed along the Pacific coast of the Americas
1581	17-year-old Galileo Galilei (1564–1642) attends services at the Cathedral of Pisa, times movements of a swinging chandelier with his pulse and concludes some things about the nature of a pendulum; goes home and sets up his own experiment to verify
1582	Gregorian calendar adopted
1583	Dutch mathematician, Simon Stevin (1548–1620), begins studies that found the modern science of hydrostatics
1585	Walter Raleigh (1554–1618) attempts settlement on Roanoke Island, now in North Carolina
1586	Stevin makes some tests with falling rocks (less scientific than Galileo's)
1589	Galileo starts a series of tests to measure falling bodies
1589	William Lee, English clergyman, invents the stocking frame, the first knitting machine (early hint of the Industrial Revolution to come)
1590	Dutch spectacle maker Zacharias Janssen perfects the microscope
1596–1650	René Descartes, French philosopher and champion of rational thinking who founded analytical geometry and made extensive contributions to the philosophy of science

1597	German alchemist Andreas Liebau (Libavius) publishes the *Alchemia*, summerizing medieval achievements in alchemy. Written clearly, not mystically, it is generally considered to be the first chemical textbook; sets stage for the birth of chemistry 60 years later
1600	William Gilbert publishes *De magnete* ("About magnets") describing results of his experiments with magnetism; concludes the Earth itself is a huge magnet
1600	Italian philosopher and mystic Giordano Bruno (born 1548) is burned at the stake
1603	Italian physician Hieronymus Fabricius (1537–1619) studies valves in veins and speculates that blood in the veins of the legs moves only toward the heart, but he does not publish, not wanting to contradict Galen
1607	John Smith settles Jamestown settlement in Virginia, first permanent English settlement in the Americas
1608	Dutch spectacle maker Hans Lippershey begins working on telescope
1609	Kepler works out planetary orbits; Galileo studies Milky Way and the Moon with telescope of his own devising
1610	French colony established in Quebec
1610	Galileo studies Jupiter and its four visible moons; also Venus and sunspots
1611	Publication of the King James translation of the Bible
1614	Italian physician Santorio Santorio, known as Sanctorius (1561–1636), studies metabolism, builds elaborate weighing machine for measuring input and output
1616	English playwright William Shakespeare dies the same day (April 23) as Spanish writer Miguel de Cervantes
1618	The Thirty Years' War, a conflict between Protestants and Catholics, begins in Germany and spreads to neighboring countries
1620	English philosopher Francis Bacon publishes his arguments for the scientific method
1620	Pilgrims land at Plymouth Rock in what is now Massachusetts
1624	Flemish physician Jan Baptista van Helmont (1579–1644) begins work with vapors and gases

1627	Kepler publishes a book of planetary tables
1628	Harvey publishes his book *De Motus Cordis* on motions of the heart and blood
1633	Galileo is condemned by the Church
1636	Harvard College is founded in Massachusetts
1637	Descartes publishes his *Discours sur la méthode*
1642	Pascal, a French mathematician and philosopher (1623–62) invents a calculating machine
1642	English Civil War begins
1643	Louis XIV becomes king of France
1645	German physicist Otto von Guericke invents air pump—enables experiments in a vacuum
1648	Thirty Years' War ends
1649	Charles I of England is beheaded
1650	Anglican bishop James Ussher dates the creation at 4004 B.C. (We now know that early humans were on Earth at least 2.4 million years ago)
1654	Pascal and Fermat lay foundations for probability theory
1656	Christiaan Huygens (1629–95) studies Saturn's rings and discovers Saturn's moon Titan; builds first pendulum clock
1657	Robert Hooke (1635–1703) perfects an air pump and runs experiments in a vacuum with a feather and a coin to test Galileo's theory
1658	Dutch naturalist Jan Swammerdam, one of first experimenters with microscopes, father of modern entomology, discovers the red blood corpuscle
1658	Oliver Cromwell dies, ending the reign of his government in England
1660	Restoration of the kingdom in England
1660	Marcello Malpighi (1628–94), pioneer microscopist, discovers capillaries
1660	Guericke discovers static electricity (first to demonstrate it on large scale)
1661	Irish-born physicist and chemist Robert Boyle (1627–91) publishes the *Skeptical Chymist*
1662	Boyle gets Hooke to build improved air pump and develops Boyle's law regarding gases—results in strongest evidence yet for ancient ideas of atomism
1662	The Royal Society, an organization devoted to science, is founded in England

1664	Hooke discovers and studies the Great Red Spot on Jupiter
1665	Hooke publishes *Micrographia* on his work with a microscope
1665	Giovanni Domenico Cassini (1625–1712) determines the rotation speed of Mars
1665	The plague hits London and Cambridge, forcing Isaac Newton to retreat to his family's farm
1665	Posthumous work of Italian physicist Francesco Maria Grimaldi (1618–63) is published, demonstrating the principles of light refraction
1666	English scientist Isaac Newton (1642–1727) works on problems of light and spectrum
1668	Francesco Redi (Italian physician, 1626–97) does studies that (at least for the moment) lay to rest ancient theories of spontaneous generation
1668	Newton invents a reflecting telescope
1669	Newton and Gottfried Wilhelm Leibniz (1646–1716) independently develop calculus
1669	Danish geologist Nicolaus Steno (1638–86) maintains that fossils are remains of ancient creatures
1671	Giovanni Cassini discovers seventh moon of Saturn and will discover three more over the next 13 years
1672	Giovanni Cassini determines the distance of Mars from Earth (first inkling of the vastness of space)
1675	Danish astronomer Olaus Roemer (1644–1710) calculates the speed of light
1676	Dutch microscopist Antony van Leeuwenhoek (1632–1723) makes best microscopes of the time, capable of 200x magnification; discovers living microorganisms in dirty rain water and pond water (he calls them "animalcules")
1677	Leeuwenhoek discovers spermatozoa in semen
1678	Newton's studies lead him to believe that light is composed of particles; Huygens's studies lead him to believe that light is waves. A battle begins to rage
1678	Edmund Halley (1656–1742) makes astronomical observations (especially of the Magellanic Clouds) from the island of St. Helena, in the south Atlantic Ocean; publishes a star catalog (more than 300 stars that had not been included before, because he made his observations from the southern hemisphere)

1682	English botanist Nehemiah Grew (1641–1712) shows that plants reproduce sexually and that individual grains of pollen are like the sperm cells of the animal world
1683	Leeuwenhoek observes bacteria (which he recognizes as living microorganisms, although he does not know what they are exactly)
1684	Jean Picard (1620–82), French astronomer, in posthumous work gives the most accurate measurement yet for the size of the Earth
1685	Louis XIV revokes the Edict of Nantes, retracting the religious freedom that had been allowed to French Protestants (Huguenots)
1686	English naturalist John Ray (1627–1705) publishes the first of his three-volume classification of plant species
1687	Newton's laws of motion published in his book *Principia mathematica*
1689	Peter the Great becomes czar of Russia
1689	William and Mary of Orange are declared joint sovereigns of England by Parliament
1691	John Ray begins to work on a classification of animals similar to the one he did on plants
1693	Leibniz invents a better calculating machine than Pascal's
1698	Halley commands the ship the *Paramour Pink* in a two-year sea expedition measuring magnetic declinations all over the world and determining latitude and longitude for ports at which he stops. First charter of a ship for sole purposes of scientific investigation
1704	Newton's *Opticks* is published; becomes standard textbook in the study of light for the rest of the 18th century

G L O S S A R Y

a posteriori reasoning inductive reasoning, arriving at conclusions derived by reasoning from observed facts

a priori reasoning deductive reasoning, reasoning from the general to the particular

acceleration any change in velocity, that is, any change in direction or speed, or both

air resistance the slowing effect air has on anything passing through it, due to friction

alchemy the practice (which has never succeeded) of trying to turn other metals into gold; alchemists were the earliest chemists

aorta the large artery carrying blood away from the heart

artery one of the blood vessels that carries blood away from the heart to the extremities

astrology the practice of predicting the outcome of human events based on the supposed influences of the stars and planets, their positions and aspects

bestiary a medieval work on the habits and types of animals, both real and imaginary, often taking an allegorical and moralizing tone

Bronze Age the period from 3500 to 1000 B.C., when people first developed and used bronze tools and implements

capillary one of the blood vessels with a slender opening the size of a hair that join the ends of arteries to the ends of veins

comet sometimes called a "dirty snowball," a celestial body composed of ice and rock whose orbit around the Sun may take it far out to the edge of the Solar System as well as very close to the Sun, where it may develop a bright, gaseous tail

cosmology a branch of astronomy that deals with the origin of the universe, its structure and space-time relationships

cosmos an orderly harmonious systematic universe

cuneiform composed or written in wedge-shaped characters, often used when writing on clay tablets

deductive reasoning a priori reasoning, a process of reasoning that establishes general truths first, and then moves to particular instances

dissection procedure to expose the parts, for instance, of an organism, for scientific examination

elliptical having the shape of a curve made in such a way that the sum of its distances from two fixed points is a constant—forming a somewhat flattened circle

embryo the earliest stages of growth of an animal prior to birth; in humans the stage between the fertilized egg and the fetus

entomologist a specialist in insects

epicycle in Ptolemaic astronomy, the small circle in which a planet was believed to move uniformly at the same time as the epicycle's center traveled along the circumference of a larger circle around the Earth

ether (not the anesthetic), in the ancient Greek sense the transparent substance believed to permeate the whole universe, carrying light. No one could ever detect it, though, and two scientists, Albert Michelson and Edward Morley, finally showed in an experiment they performed in 1887 that ether does not exist

falsifiable possible to prove untrue

focus (plural, foci) the center of a circle, or in the case of an ellipse, one of the two central points around which it is constructed

geocentric with the Earth at the center

heliocentric with the Sun at the center

herbal a book about plants, especially those used for medicinal purposes

hieroglyph a character used in a hieroglyphic or pictorial system of writing, such as the one used by the ancient Egyptian priesthood

humanism the revival of interest in classical literature and art, the increase in individualism and critical spirit and an emphasis on nonreligious concerns that was characteristic of the Renaissance

humor (as in four humors) one of the four fluids which, according to medieval physiology, constituted the body; according to this idea, the relative proportion of these humors—bile, blood, phlegm and melancholy or black bile—determined a person's health and temperament

hypothesis a tentative assumption made in order to draw out and test its logical or empirical consequences; formulation of a natural principle based on inference from observed data (see also *theory* and *law*)

inclined plane a tipped, flat surface, such as a ramp

inductive reasoning a posteriori reasoning, a process of reasoning that establishes general truths based on particular instances

law in science, a statement of an order or relation of phenomena that so far as is known is invariable under the given conditions (see also *theory* and *hypothesis*)

ligation tying off or binding, for example, to stop or slow the flow of blood through a vein or artery

light year the distance light travels in a vacuum in one year, about 5.878 billion miles

maria (plural of mare) literally, "seas," a term used to describe the large, dark areas on the surface of the Moon

mean the arithmetical average, computed by dividing the sum of a group of terms by the number of terms

metallurgy the science and technology of metals

microscope an arrangement of lenses that magnifies to a visible level things so small that they are invisible to the naked eye

Neolithic age the New Stone Age (see also *New Stone Age*)

New Stone Age the Neolithic age, from about 8000 B.C. to about 4000 B.C., when early humans developed agriculture, began domesticating animals and started making pottery

nova a star that suddenly increases its light output dramatically, fading back to its normal relative dimness in a few months or years

objective as opposed to subjective, applied to reports or observations, indicating that personal opinions or prejudices have not been included; based on repeatable experiments and falsifiable data

Old Stone Age period during which early humans began using stone tools and implements, extending back perhaps as far as 1.4 million years (compare to the *Neolithic* or *New Stone Age*)

paradigm a system of interlocking facts, theories and philosophies so widely accepted that it becomes implicitly accepted as a basis for thinking about scientific problems. When new discoveries call an old paradigm into question, the resulting restructuring of theories and philosophies into a new paradigm is known as a paradigm shift

planet for the ancients, any of the bodies of matter in the sky—the Sun, Moon, Venus, Jupiter, and so on—that seemed to have motions of their own against the backdrop of seemingly fixed stars. Today just those bodies traveling in orbits around the Sun, with the exception of satellites, comets and asteroids, are called planets

prism a solid, transparent object with identical bases and whose sides are all parallelograms; when light shines through a prism it separates into its spectrum

projectile anything impelled forward, for instance, flung, thrown or shot, such as a rock or an arrow

quantify to express an idea or concept in terms of numbers

rarefaction in physics, the decrease of pressure and density in a medium, such as air, expanding without adding any additional matter

Reformation a 16th-century religious movement marked by upheaval and rejection by some groups of Roman Catholic doctrine and authority and resulting in the establishment of Protestant churches

Renaissance a transitional period in Europe between medieval and modern times, beginning in Italy in the 14th century and lasting until the 17th century, marked by a humanistic revival of interest in classical philosophy and arts, a flowering of the arts, and the beginnings of modern science

retrograde motion of celestial bodies, a motion contrary to the motion of similar bodies

retrogression movement in a reverse or retrograde direction

"save the phenomena" as used by the ancient Greeks, an expression meaning to adjust a theory so that it does not conflict with observations

scholasticism a philosophical movement dominant in the western Christian tradition from the 9th until the 17th century, marked by strict adherence to dogma and traditional authority

septum (heart) the dividing membrane between two chambers of the heart

Solar System the system of planets revolving around the Sun

subjective as opposed to objective, applied to reports or observations, indicating that the observer/reporter's personal opinions or prejudices color his or her statements

supernova one of the rarely observed nova outbursts in which the maximum intrinsic luminosity reaches as high as 100 million times that of the Sun

teleology the idea, based on a misinterpretation of Aristotle, that future events control the present, that is, that "A is so in order that B might be so," that nature or natural processes are directed toward an end or shaped by a purpose

telescope an arrangement of lenses and mirrors in a tube that makes distant objects appear nearer

theory in science, a plausible or scientifically acceptable principle or body of principles offered to explain phenomena (see also *hypothesis* and *law*)

vacuum a space containing absolutely no matter

vein one of the blood vessels that carries blood toward the heart from the extremities

velocity the rate at which a body moves in a given direction; when physicists speak of velocity they refer not only to the speed at which an object moves, but also to the direction in which it is moving

vena cava the large vein running to the heart

vivisection to perform a dissection on a living organism (animal or plant)

F U R T H E R
R E A D I N G

ABOUT SCIENCE:

Cole, K. C. *Sympathetic Vibrations: Reflections on Physics as a Way of Life*. New York: William Morrow, 1985. Well written, lively and completely intriguing look at physics presented in a thoughtful and insightful way by a writer who cares for her subject. The emphasis here is primarily modern physics, concentrating more on the ideas than the history.

Ferris, Timothy, ed. *The World Treasury of Physics, Astronomy and Mathematics*. New York: Little, Brown, 1991. Anthology of mostly modern physics but includes some general papers on the philosophy of science as well as some delightful poetry on physics. Sometimes difficult but well worth browsing through.

Fisher, David E. *The Creation of the Universe*. Indianapolis: Bobbs-Merrill, 1977. Easy-to-follow, enthusiastic narrative aimed at the younger reader.

Fleisher, Paul. *Secrets of the Universe: Discovering the Universal Laws*. New York: Atheneum, 1987. Well-written and engrossing look at physics aimed at the younger reader but enjoyable and informative for anyone interested in science. Includes excellent discussions of the work of Galileo, Newton and others, as well as general laws of physics.

Gonick, Larry, and Art Huffman. *The Cartoon Guide to Physics*. New York: Harper Perennial, 1991. Fun, but the whiz-bang approach sometimes zips by important points a little too fast.

Hann, Judith. *How Science Works*. Pleasantville, N.Y.: Reader's Digest, 1991. Lively well illustrated look at physics for young readers. Good, brief explanations of basic laws and short historical overviews accompany many easy experiments readers can perform.

Hazen, Robert M., and James Trefil. *Science Matters: Achieving Scientific Literacy*. New York: Doubleday, 1991. A clear and readable overview of basic principles of science and how they apply to science in today's world.

Holzinger, Philip R. *House of Science*. New York: John Wiley & Sons, 1990. Lively question-and-answer discussion of science for young adults. Includes activities and experiments.

Morrison, Philip, and Phylis Morrison. *The Ring of Truth: An Inquiry into How We Know What We Know*. New York: Random House, 1987. Companion to the PBS television series. Wonderful and highly personal explanations of science and the scientific process. Easy to read and engrossing.

Rensberger, Boyce. *How the World Works: A Guide To Science's Greatest Discoveries*. New York: William Morrow, 1986. Lucid and readable explanations of major scientific concepts, terms explained in A-to-Z format, and excellent discussions of the scientific method and how science works.

Trefil, James. *1001 Things Everyone Should Know about Science*. New York: Doubleday, 1992. Just what the title says—and well done.

Walker, Jearl. *The Flying Circus of Physics with Answers*. New York: John Wiley & Sons, 1977. By now a classic collection of problems and questions about physics in the everyday world. Little history but much fun.

ABOUT THE HISTORY OF SCIENCE:

Asimov, Isaac. *Asimov's Chronology of Science and Discovery*. New York: Harper and Row, 1989. Lively chronological view of science, year by year. Written with Asimov's usual verve. Good for fact-checking and browsing.

Boorstin, Daniel J. *The Discoverers*. New York: Random House, 1983. Its size may be intimidating—over 700 pages—but this is a wonderfully lively, thoughtful and absorbing look at the history of humankind's search to know itself and nature. Aimed at the general reader.

Brooke, John Hedley. *Science and Religion: Some Historical Perspectives*. Cambridge: Cambridge University Press, 1991. This higher-level book is sometimes difficult, but it gives a well presented and insightful look at the relationship between science and religion throughout history.

Gillespie, Charles C. *The Edge of Objectivity*. Princeton: Princeton University Press, 1960. Intriguing higher-level look at science, its history and philosophy.

Hays, H. R. *Birds, Beasts, and Men: A Humanist History of Zoology*. New York: G. P. Putnam's Sons, 1972. Readable and well-organized narrative, but old and may be hard to find.

Hellemans, Alexander, and Bryan Bunch. *The Timetables of Science.* New York: Simon and Schuster, 1988. An easy-to-read, year-by-year chronology of science. Good for fact-finding or just browsing. And the "overviews" are nicely done, adding historical context.

Magner, Lois N. *A History of the Life Sciences.* New York: Marcell Dekker, 1979. A good, readable overview though marred somewhat by awkward organization.

Mason, Stephen F. *A History of the Sciences*, revised edition. New York: Collier Books, 1962. Originally published in 1956, this book is older than Ronan's history (below) but is a solid standard history of science.

Ronan, Colin. *The Atlas of Scientific Discovery.* New York: Crescent Books, 1983. A slim coffeetable book but well written and thought-out overview with illustrations.

Ronan, Colin A. *Science: Its History and Development Among the World's Cultures.* New York: Facts On File, 1982. A good, readable comprehensive overview of the history of science from the ancients to the present.

Sambursky, S. *The Physical World of the Greeks.* Princeton: Princeton University Press, 1956. Reprinted in paperback, 1987. For the reader wishing to delve much more in detail into the classic physics of the great Greek philosophers. Tough going in spots for the younger or general reader.

ABOUT THE SCIENTIFIC REVOLUTION AND ITS TIME:

Butterfield, H. J. *The Origins of Modern Science: 1300–1800.* New York: Macmillan, 1958. A highly regarded standard history. Older but still dependable and insightful.

Cohen, I. Bernard. *The Newtonian Revolution.* Cambridge: Cambridge University Press, 1983. A standard work.

Hall, A. Rupert. *From Galileo to Newton.* New York: Dover, 1981. Good, solid and dependable, though sometimes a little dry.

Kuhn, Thomas S. *The Copernican Revolution.* New York: Random House, 1957. Classic, once-controversial sociological look at the Copernican Revolution. Somewhat difficult reading.

Sarton, George. *Six Wings: Men of Science in the Renaissance.* Bloomington: Indiana University Press, 1957. This classic conveys a good feel for the period.

ABOUT SCIENTISTS:

Abbott, David, ed. *The Biographical Dictionary of Scientists: Astronomers.* New York: Peter Bedrick Books, 1984. Short entries from A to Z, including an extensive glossary and line diagrams. Dry and a little difficult, but a good resource.

————. *The Biographical Dictionary of Scientists: Physicists.* New York: Peter Bedrick Books, 1984. Like Abbott's dictionary of astronomers, a reliable reference, though somewhat tough going.

Armitage, Angus. *Copernicus: The Founder of Modern Astronomy.* New York: Dorset Press, 1990. Awkwardly written, but informative.

Asimov, Isaac. *Asimov's Biographical Encyclopedia of Science and Technology,* second revised edition. Garden City, N.Y.: Doubleday, 1982. The somewhat unusual chronological and nonalphabetical entry system takes some getting used to, but overall a lively and typically opinionated Asimov approach makes for fascinating reading as well as basic fact gathering.

Banville, John. *Kepler, A Novel.* Boston: David R. Godine, 1984. Historically accurate, challenging and absorbing novel based on Kepler's life and his relationship to Tycho Brahe.

Christianson, Gale E. *This Wild Abyss: The Story of the Men Who Made Modern Astronomy.* New York: Free Press (Division of Macmillan), 1978. Easy-to-read narrative history of astronomy.

Cobb, Vicki. *Truth on Trial: The Story of Galileo Galilei.* Illustrated by George Ulrich. New York: Coward, McCann and Geoghegan, 1979. Written as a story for young readers, slim but easy to read.

Galilei, Galileo. *Discoveries and Opinions of Galileo,* translated, with introduction and notes, by Stillman Drake. New York: Anchor Books/Doubleday, 1957. Young students and readers will be surprised to find how lively and provocative Galileo's writing was for its time, and how well it stands up today. Drake's comments and notes add context and occasional clarification but it is Galileo who steals the show in this surprisingly fresh book.

Keele, Kenneth D. *William Harvey: The Man, the Physician and the Scientist.* London: Thomas Nelson and Sons, 1965.

Marcus, Rebecca B. *William Harvey: Trailblazer of Scientific Medicine.* New York: Franklin Watts, 1962. Well written and easy to read, although some explanations are not clear.

Meadows, Jack. *The Great Scientists.* New York: Oxford University Press, 1987. Easy to read, well presented and nicely illustrated. Available in paperback.

INDEX

Boldface type indicates major topics. *Italic* type indicates illustrations.

INDEX

astronomy *See* comets; Copernican system;
  cosmology; nova; planetary motion;
  Ptolemaic system; supernova
atomism 12–13, 28, 138, 145
Averroës 25–26, 140
Avicenna 83
Ayurveda (Hindu text) 28

B

Babylonians 5–7, 6, 20, 137
Bacon, Francis viii, 28, 68–69, 142, 144
Bacon, Roger 54, 111–112
bacteria 121, 147
barber-surgeons 85, 89–90, 141
Bennewitz, Peter 142
bestiaries 123, 126, 126–128, 133, 149
Biblia naturae (Bible of Nature) (Jan
  Swammerdam) 116
biology *See* anatomy; classification of living
  things; pharmacology; physiology
blood and circulation 99–110
  ancient views of 11, 15
  Fabricius discovery of valves in veins
    90, 103–104, 107, 144
  Galen theories on 82, 99–103, 107
  Harvey study of 103–110, 145
  Malpighi discovery of capilaries 111,
    113, 115, 120, 145
  mechanistic theory 135–136
  Swammerdam discovery of red
    corpuscle 145
  Vesalius dissection of animals 87,
    102–103
blood-letting 107
blood transfusions 109
Boch, Jerome 128
Boral, Pierre 112
Borelli, Giovanni 113–114
botany 15, 115, 128 *See also* herbals
Boyle, Robert 71, 104, 109, 145
Boyle's law 145
Brahe, Tycho *See* Tycho
brain 11, 82, 95, 100
bronze 4–5
Bronze Age 5–6, 149
Brunfels, Otto 128
Bruno, Giordano 61, 144
bubonic plague 67, 139–140
Buridan, Jean 28, 58

C

Calcar, Jan Stephen van 87
calculating machine 145, 147
calculus 67, 76, 146
calendar 5, 137
Calvin, John 102, 141
Cambridge University 67, 103
capillaries 113, 115, 120, 145, 149
cassava plant 5

Cassegrain, Guillaume 74
Cassini, Giovanni Domenico 146
catapult 25
Causes and Cures (St. Hildegard the Nun)
  128
cauterization 90
cells 116
Central America 5
Chang Heng (Zhang Heng) 29, 139
Châtelet, Emilie du 76, 77
chemistry *See* alchemy; pharmacology;
  physiology
China 29
  alchemy 91
  astronomy
    comets 43
    nova observations 139
    solar eclipse 139
    solar year length 139
  geology 140
  magnetism 54
  mapmaking 139
  rocketry 140
  weather records 137
Christian IV, king of Denmark 44
Christian church *See also* Church of
  England; Protestantism; Roman Catholic
  church
  astrology opposed by 20
  as barrier to direct study of nature
    27–28
  bestiaries used for moral instruction 127
  Copernicus tolerated by 40
  fossils as challenge to 129
  Galen popular with 82, 100
  humans seen as centerpiece of creation
    36
chromatic aberration 118–119
Chu Hsi (Zhu Xi) 29, 140
Church of England 66
chyle 100
circulatory system *See* blood and circulation
classification of living things 123–133
  Aristotle 125, 127–128, 131
  Dioscorides 125–126
  Gesner 128–131
  Ray 131–133, 147
  species 131–133, 147
coffee 103
College of Cardinals *See* Roman Catholic
  church
Columbo, Realdo 102
Columbus, Christopher 33, 65, 141
comets 43, 74, 141–143, 149
compass *See* magnetic compass
condom 90
Copernican system 38–41, 39
  Galileo and 52, 57, 59–63, 62
  Gilbert and 55
  Kepler and 45–46

160

INDEX

Newton 67, 72
 Sanctorius 97
 laws of motion vii, 53, 56–59, 57
 legacy 135
 opposition to 109
 scientific method 53–54, 65, 69, 106
 telescope 47, 57, 59–60, 62–63, 112, 120, 144
 at University of Padua 56, 104
 writings 58, 60–62, 62
Gamba, Marina 53
geocentric (earth-centered) system See Copernican system
geology 29
geometry
 Apollonius of Perga 19
 Archimedes 24
 Descartes 69, 143
 early developments 137
 Euclid 19, 138
 Pythagoras 10, 137
germ theory 94
Gesner, Konrad 112, **128–131**
Gilbert, William 47, **54–55**, 69, 142, 144
gold, turning base metals into See alchemy
grave-robbery 85
gravity viii, 25, 73
 Newton's apple 67
Great Chain of Being 125
Great Red Spot (Jupiter) 146
Greeks See also individual thinkers
 classical period 3, 6–17, 137–138
 Hellenistic period 19–25, 138–139
 medieval reverence for 28, 139–140
Gregory, Bruce 47
Gregory, James 74
Grew, Nehemiah 115, 122, 147
Grimaldi, Francesco Maria 146
Guericke, Otto von 145
gunpowder 29
Gustavus Adolphus 56

H

Halley, Edmund 71–72, 76, 146–147
Halley's Comet 74
Harmonices Mundi (Harmonies of the World) (Johannes Kepler) 47
Harvey, William **103–110**, 105
 completion of work by Malpighi 111, 113
 conservatism of 102
 legacy of 135
 predecessors 99–103
 writings 105–106, 108, 145
heart See blood and circulation
heliocentric (sun-centered) system See Copernican system
Hellenic World 19
Helmont, Jan Baptista van 98, 132, 144

Heraclitus of Ephesus 11, 137
herbals 123–126, 124, 150
hieroglyphs 5–6, 150
Hildegard, Saint See St. Hildegard the Nun
Hipparchus of Nicea 19–22, 21, 139
Hippocrates 27, 98, 100
Hippocratic Oath 97, 98
Histoires (Histories) (Bovier Fontenelle) 70
Historia animalium (History of Animals) (Konrad Gesner) 128–129, 130
Hobbes, Thomas 63
hollow-pipe construction 56
honeybee 116
Hooke, Robert **116**
 air pump 71, 109, 145
 conflict with Newton 76, 116
 fossil theory 129
 Jupiter feature discovery 146
 legacy of 122
 light and optics 68, 75, 116
 microscope 112, 116
 planetary motion 71–72
 writings 68, 116, 117, 146
humanism 35, 47, 150 See also Renaissance
humors (physiological theory) 94, 97, 150
Huygens, Christiaan 70–71, 75–76, 145–146
hydrostatic balance 56
hydrostatics 143
hypothesis ix, viii, 48, 150

I

iatrochemistry See pharmacology
idealism 138
impetus 58
inclined plane vii, 57–58, 150
India **28–29**, 138
inductive reasoning 68–69, 149, 151
Industrial Revolution 69
inertia 72–73
Inquisition See Roman Catholic church
"insensible perspiration" 97
"inverse square" law 71–72
iron, smelting of 6
Islam 26

J

Janssen, Zacharias 112, 143
Japan 29, 43, 139
Jupiter (planet)
 Great Red Spot 146
 liver influenced by (Paracelsus) 95
 moons of 47, 60, 144
 in Ptolemaic system 22
 retrograde motion of 38–39

Ivn

3/03 11/02

—, 13, 29   1993   11/6